Routledge Revivals

The Extra Year

First Published in 1970, *The Extra Year* discusses the raising of the school leaving age, a crucial event in British education. It is also highly controversial: its repercussions affected teachers, educationists, parents and employers as well as pupils themselves. Each of the contributors to this book examines one aspect of its implications. After a general introduction by Professor Tibble, Malcolm Seaborn looks at the historical background of the decision to raise the school leaving age and Professor Eggleston considers some of its sociological aspects. Professor Tibble then examines the ways in which the situation will affect pupils and their teachers, John Sheehan discusses some economic factors and Tyrrell Burgess looks at the implications for further education. The headmaster's point of view is given by Albert Rowe and probable changes in the school curriculum are analyzed by Dennis Lawton. A final chapter by Professor McAulay discusses American experience. This is an important historical reference work for students and scholars of education.

The Extra Year
The Raising of the School Leaving Age

Edited by J. W. Tibble

First published in 1970
by Routledge & Kegan Paul Ltd.

This edition first published in 2024 by Routledge
4 Park Square, Milton Park, Abingdon, Oxon, OX14 4RN

and by Routledge
605 Third Avenue, New York, NY 10017

Routledge is an imprint of the Taylor & Francis Group, an informa business

© 1970 Routledge & Kegan Paul Ltd.

All rights reserved. No part of this book may be reprinted or reproduced or utilised in any form or by any electronic, mechanical, or other means, now known or hereafter invented, including photocopying and recording, or in any information storage or retrieval system, without permission in writing from the publishers.

Publisher's Note
The publisher has gone to great lengths to ensure the quality of this reprint but points out that some imperfections in the original copies may be apparent.

Disclaimer
The publisher has made every effort to trace copyright holders and welcomes correspondence from those they have been unable to contact.

A Library of Congress record exists under ISBN: 0710068832

ISBN: 978-1-032-79371-9 (hbk)
ISBN: 978-1-003-49168-2 (ebk)
ISBN: 978-1-032-79372-6 (pbk)

Book DOI 10.4324/9781003491682

The extra year

The raising of the school leaving age

Edited by
J. W. Tibble
Emeritus Professor of Education
University of Leicester

London Routledge & Kegan Paul

*First published in 1970
by Routledge & Kegan Paul Ltd
Broadway House, 68–74 Carter Lane
London E.C.4
Printed in Great Britain by
Ebenezer Baylis & Son Ltd
The Trinity Press, Worcester, and London*
© *Routledge & Kegan Paul Ltd.* 1970
*No part of this book may be reproduced
in any form without permission from
the publisher except for the quotation
of brief passages in criticism*

ISBN 0 7100 6883 2 (c)
0 7100 6884 0 (p)

Contents

Introduction
J. W. Tibble *Emeritus Professor of Education, University of Leicester*   1

1 **The historical background**
Malcolm Seaborne *Senior Lecturer in Education, University of Leicester*   9

2 **Some sociological considerations**
S. J. Eggleston *Professor of Education, University of Keele*   20

3 **The pupils and their teachers**
J. W. Tibble   37

4 **Economic aspects**
John Sheehan *Lecturer in Political Economy, University College, Dublin*   55

5 **The further education option**
Tyrrell Burgess *Research Fellow, Higher Education Research Unit, London School of Economics*   70

6 **A headmaster's point of view**
Albert Rowe *Headmaster, David Lister High School, Hull*   83

7 **Preparations for changes in the curriculum**
Denis Lawton, *Senior Lecturer in Curriculum Studies, University of London Institute of Education*   97

8 **An American viewpoint**
J. D. McAulay *Professor of Education, Pennsylvania State University*   117

Introduction

J. W. Tibble

In this book a number of contributors concerned with education were asked to consider, each from a particular point of view, the implications of the impending raising of the school leaving age to 16. It might be thought desirable that an assessment of the educational implications of a policy decision of this order should be made well in advance of the decision, so that the consequences of the change can be foreseen and as far as possible prepared for. However, feasibility studies and the assessment of alternative procedures are not yet common practice in educational matters. As Mr Seaborne comments at the end of Chapter 1, considering the record of the last century, 'we may conclude that it shows all too often that educational advances take place for non-educational reasons and almost, one might say, by stealth'.

The politics of education, the definition of the factors which influence political decisions concerning education, is not yet a very well-defined or precise field of study, except as an aspect of educational history. We can, at any rate, look back at earlier decisions concerning compulsory education and the length of compulsory schooling and consider the circumstances in which they were made and the consequences of the change of policy. This is what the first chapter is about, and one of the main conclusions Mr Seaborne reaches has already been noted. There is nothing very specific or precise, certainly not in terms of educational benefits or consequences, which motivates the decisions. It is almost as if they were made by a process of extrapolation with reference to past trends, 'an element of inevitability', Mr Seaborne calls it. It is, of course, easy to understand, in retrospect, that once it had become accepted in the nineteenth century that a minimum of formal education was essential for all citizens of a democratic, industrialized society, the door was opened for progressive extensions of that minimum to meet the needs of both individuals and society in an expanding economy. Education creates needs, as well as satisfying them. There is no logical termination of this process, or indeed physiological or psychological, short of senility. A scholar may be, according to context, a young child or a don of ripe years.

One who continues his education into adult years, however, does so voluntarily. We are concerned in this book with compulsory education, and what we have to be aware of is that, at some point in between childhood and adulthood, education and compulsion may become contradictory processes. For young people who see no value in their present schooling, who are impatient to leave school, earn money, acquire status in the adult world, the compulsory extra year may well be mis-educative, a sterile period of marking time. It is generally recognized that this, apart from the wastefulness to the individual concerned, could create serious problems for the schools in which they are prisoners.

On the other hand, we have to recognize, as Mr Seaborne also points out with regard to earlier extensions of the school leaving age, the educational benefits, however little foreseen or planned, which did in fact accrue were considerable. The changes led to reappraisals of aims, improvements in organization and facilities and, in the case of the last extension to 15, a striking increase in the numbers of children staying on after that age.

Professor Eggleston explores in some detail the sociological factors involved in these changes and the implications of the extension to 16. In responding to and meeting the needs of the stayers-on – mainly those likely to achieve some success in traditional academic courses – the schools have unintentionally created another subculture of those for whom these courses, and the examination incentives associated with them, are made less appropriate. The term 'delinquescent' has been coined to describe this subculture, since, in relation to the official objectives and ethos of the school, its members feel themselves and often are felt to be by the staff opters-out, noncomformists and often anti-authority and antagonistic. Sociological studies of schools, both in terms of their internal organization and of their relations with other institutions, have been carried out in recent years which throw light on problems like this, and should enable us in the future to estimate more accurately the educational consequences of the ways schools are organized. It seems evident enough that a system which insists on labelling about half its members as inferior and which condemns them to continuous failure does not provide the best incentives for these pupils, either for learning or for identification with the school and its values and objectives. Professor Eggleston stresses the need for changes which could enable all pupils

> to see the school as offering a range of acceptable and legitimate activity like that which students at colleges of further education universities and technical colleges tend to experience. Such a relationship is frankly contractual. It is not an easy one to relate to the compulsory attendance regime that would follow the raising of the school leaving age, but it is by no means impossible to do so as many industrial training schemes demonstrate. But it is certainly unlikely that it could incorporate the commitment to a set of school-imposed values that is still the model of many educators. Indeed, it is unlikely that the school will ever again have almost undisputed power to impose a set of school values upon its total adolescent population.

That seems to me to be close to the crux of the matter, and the success or failure of the extra year in terms of benefit or boredom for at least half the age-group staying on depends very much on whether the schools and teachers concerned can accept that diagnosis and its implications. In Chapter 3 I explore the more psychological implications, particularly the assumptions and attitudes built into the models teachers use in the organization of schools, the nature of the curriculum and methods of teaching and learning. This leads to the general conclusion that changes in curricular content and methods which are not accompanied by changes in the nature of the relationships between teachers and pupils are not likely to be successful in the case of the young people referred to in *Half Our Future*. This kind of change is, of course, asking a great deal of the teachers concerned. They know how to operate the traditional model with considerable success and for growing numbers of children. It is the one they themselves were brought up in and have been successful in working to, from both sides of the fence. We are asking those who are concerned with the present school-leavers and the new compulsory stayers-on to operate on a different set of basic assumptions and work out a different kind of relationship with these pupils. It is all the harder because the new assumptions and attitudes are in a sense the opposites of the prevailing ones (at any rate in secondary education): listening instead of holding forth; learning with instead of instructing; helping pupils to find incentives instead of assuming that carrots will do and that the only alternative to carrots is sticks; being able to tolerate negative and unco-operative attitudes from pupils without feeling these as dire threats to the teacher's authority and as personal affronts. It is clear that teachers are going to need a good deal of support and help if they are to find it possible to make these changes in themselves. I go so far as to say this should be recognized as a priority for in-service education, and as many short courses as possible specially designed to help teachers to acquire the new skills and attitudes. One could say that these skills and attitudes are akin to those normally acquired in the training of a social worker, rather than those normally acquired by those training to be secondary teachers: except that the teacher has to apply them in the context of relatively large groups of twenty or more.

The most obvious limits on the apparently inevitable expansion of education referred to in Chapter 1 are those set by economic factors: or, rather, by arguments which refer to economic factors for their justification. As we are all aware, the earlier date for raising the age to 16 was postponed because of the economic situation in 1968. The White Paper of that year was concerned only with the saving in terms of public expenditure, mainly in the form of building programmes. Clearly the economics of education contains more than this, and some of the items on both sides of the account, the costs and the gains, may be very difficult to quantify. Nevertheless, it is very important that the attempt be made, and that our present technique for doing this be improved. In Chapter 4 Mr Sheehan considers the economic aspects of the extra year without glossing over any of the complexities and problems. If the main conclusions for this survey are mainly negative, they are none the less important. Mr Sheehan certainly debunks some of the most commonly advanced general arguments which assume that automatic economic benefits will accrue. The moral is that we must be much more specific in defining educational objectives, and particularly in considering alternative procedures before decisions are reached. As Mr Sheehan says, the main reasons for a measure like raising the leaving age should be social and cultural rather than economic: nevertheless, all such changes have economic consequences, and we need as accurate a picture of these as we can get.

One of the possible alternative procedures for dealing with some of the extra year's population is considered by Mr Tyrrell Burgess in Chapter 5: this is the possibility of the extra year being optionally spent within the orbit of further education rather than within the secondary system. As Mr Burgess makes clear, the two systems are different in many respects and represent different traditions in English education; in a sense, the further education system was developed to meet the needs of those wanting education beyond the leaving age, but for whom the full-time academic education of the sixth forms was not suitable. As we shall see in earlier chapters of this book, many early-leavers who did later experience part-time further education comment favourably on the difference both in the type and content of courses, the optional setting and the different attitudes of their instructors. Of course, they may well be contributing to the change themselves by their response to voluntary as compared with compulsory education. Chapter 5 explores the possibilities and the snags: as an alternative to restricting all the extra year to the secondary sphere, it is well worth considering. It would pose administrative problems, but these should not be insoluble.

In Chapter 6 we turn again to the consequences for secondary schools. Mr Albert Rowe, writing from a headmaster's viewpoint, stresses the need for better material facilities and teacher/student ratios if the problems of the schools are to be coped with. He then makes the important point that it is a mistake to think of these as problems of the extra year only. 'The point needs stressing: the extra year (and the further education I hope will follow it) will only make sense if it is firmly based on what has gone before.' This involves consideration of the whole of the five-year course and what follows it and how best to organize the school. Mr Rowe makes out a strong case for the integrated comprehensive school, unstreamed, with a minimum of setting for some subjects and an ethos which emphasizes co-operation and cultural relativity rather than, as in the prevailing academic model, competition and a stratified curriculum for high-fliers, average types and dim-wits. He describes the school's purpose as he would put it to a first-year pupil and then underlines the implications. It involves 'a multi-dimensional view of individuals, flexible enough to embrace them in all their infinite variety and richness, and one which is not tied to any particular set of class or quasi-academic assumptions. It can therefore speak to all sorts and conditions of pupils.'

We turn now to the things actually being done to prepare for the change, and to help teachers both to be more aware of the problems and better equipped to tackle them. The Schools Council

6   J. W. Tibble

Enquiry is one example; indeed, one could say that a major difference between this raising of the leaving age and those before it is the existence of the Schools Council and all that it stands for. For the first time since the end of the nineteenth century the central government Department for Education became an agency for the sponsoring of research and inquiry and for encouraging curricular changes, with the L.E.A.s providing facilities for teachers to prepare themselves for the changes. For the first time, then, in the history of English education, the machinery exists which could prepare adequately and in advance for a major policy change. That will not in fact happen on this occasion, despite the two years or so of extra respite; the Schools Council has not been operative long enough; it has needed time to work out its general objectives and modes of operation; some devices, such as teachers' centres, are just coming into being.[1] Nevertheless, something significant has been done in the way of preparation for the change, and this, both the general background of it and an account of specific new courses, is given by Dr Denis Lawton in Chapter 7.

Finally, we have in Chapter 8 an account by Professor Jack McAulay of the situation in the U.S.A., where thirty-one states have a leaving age of 16, in four it is 17 and in five 18. Clearly, in that respect at any rate, American public education is in advance of ours, and therefore it is instructive to consider what has happened there, and what lessons might be drawn from American experience. Professor McAulay particularly stresses that the education given these young people must prepare them to cope with a rapidly changing society. 'Perhaps the most practical education is a theoretical one, because the man with a theoretical framework will comprehend the new situation, whereas the man without it has no recourse but to muddle through.' 'The young people must receive the kind of education and training opportunities suited to the changing times. They must be so prepared that they will plan for further education and re-education when their skills and technical knowledge must be updated or when their jobs disappear because of automation and economic change.' Professor McAulay goes on to deal with the problems of schooling in the large cities of America, the problem of school failure and drop-out and the question of a suitable curriculum for the extra year. All this is very relevant to our purpose: his last paragraph may fittingly be quoted here as summarizing one of the main themes of this book as a whole: 'What is taught, how it is taught, and when and where it is taught must not be based on the needs and convenience of the school, upon the

Introduction 7

comfort of the administrators or the logistics of the system. To retain youth in school the program must have meaning for those who attend.'

NOTES

1 The Association of Teachers in Technical Institutions in a statement *Education for the Future*, February 1970, comes out firmly in favour of leaving 15 year olds in school instead of allowing some to move to technical colleges to spend their last years of compulsory full-time education. But they do recommend more 'linked courses' on which children in their final year at school are sent on day or block release to a college. They also recommend that the leaving age be pushed up to 17 and then 18 as soon as feasible.

1 The historical background

Malcolm Seaborne

When the Secretary of State for Education and Science announced an extra building grant to make possible the raising of the school leaving age to 16 in 1972–3, he remarked that the proposed change was 'a major act of policy, designed to achieve for the first time in our history a full secondary education for all'.[1] Educationists inevitably refer to the historical aspect when considering major changes, and the purpose of this introductory essay is to examine the record, to comment on its salient features and to consider their effect on present policy.

It may be convenient to begin with a brief recital of the main stages by which compulsory school attendance has been achieved.[2] Universal compulsory education did not, as is still commonly assumed, begin with the Elementary Education Act of 1870. Compulsory education could not be introduced until sufficient schools had been provided, and what the Act did was to give school boards the power to make by-laws enforcing the attendance of children between the ages of 5 and 13, subject to numerous exceptions. For example, the London School Board's by-laws gave total exemption to children over 10 who had passed Standard V and half-time exemption to those who were 'beneficially and necessarily at work'. Other school boards followed suit, but many parts of the country did not have school boards, and it was not until Sandon's Act of 1876 that School Attendance Committees were created to cover such areas, with powers to enforce attendance. Four years later Mundella's Act made it obligatory for School Boards and School Attendance Committees to adopt by-laws securing full-time attendance at school for all children between 5 and 10, but children over 10 could still obtain partial or complete exemption. There was considerable variation in the regulations adopted up and down the country, and children could be exempted from attending school at 10, 11 or 12. Even in 1893, when a new Elementary Education Act was passed on this subject, the minimum age for exemption was raised only to 11, and in 1899 to 12. In 1900 local authorities were permitted to adopt by-laws raising the age of compulsory attendance (again with exemptions) from 13 to 14, but it was not until three years after Fisher's Education Act of 1918 that 14 became the universal minimum age at which a child could leave school. It took another quarter of a century to raise the age to 15, following the passing of the 1944 Education Act.

A further point is worth making about the legal age-limits of compulsory attendance adopted in the 1870 Act and subsequent legislation. It is clear that the framers of the 1870 Act were very much influenced by the Newcastle Report of 1861, which considered that 'under the present circumstances of society, a satisfactory point will have been reached when children go to the infant school at the age of 3, and from the infant school to the day school at the age of 6 or 7 and remain ... till 10, 11 or 12'. The Report quoted one of the Assistant Commissioners with approval when he suggested that 'it is quite possible to teach a child soundly and thoroughly, in a way that he shall not forget it, all that is necessary for him to possess in the shape of intellectual attainment, by the time that he is 10 years old' – by that age he should be able to 'read a common narrative', check 'a common shop bill' and follow the arguments of 'a plain Saxon sermon'.[3] Considerations such as these explain why it was that 10, 11 or 12 remained the accepted maximum age for full-time compulsory education for so long, though only partially why 5 was adopted as the statutory minimum age, a lower limit which has remained till this day. Various ages were suggested and the fixing of 5 was largely fortuitous, as Mr Szreter has recently shown.[4] Many progressive educationists at the time, however, considered that it was preferable to begin compulsion at 5 in order to protect very young children from exploitation at home; and, since it was generally accepted that children would not be able to continue long at school, many reformers felt that the sooner a start was made the better.

Technical details of this kind give us, of course, no conception of the underlying pressures at work, nor do they tell us whether certain recurrent trends have emerged over the last century which are

The historical background 11

likely to continue to affect educational policies. For it may seem *prima facie* that there is no logical limit to the age at which compulsory attendance at school or some other educational institution may be enforced in a developing economy. Are we, for example, to assume that changes in the leaving-age are merely dependent on rising standards of living, so that once 16 has been reached we can look forward, after further periods of economic advance, to it being increased to 17, 18, 19 and so on? Will another Secretary of State – perhaps at the turn of the twentieth century – be arguing the need for 'full higher education for all', made compulsory by law?

The first general point which should be made is that, in the longer perspective of the history of education, the conception of universal compulsory education for any age-group is a recent phenomenon. When we see numerous groups of children entering or leaving their schools at the beginning or end of the school day, it is worth pausing to reflect what a revolution in social habits this represents and what an effort it was, particularly in the first thirty years or so following the 1870 Act, to secure this change. Professor Bantock has reminded us that mass literacy is a recent byproduct of industrialization;[5] and so is the habit of regular attendance at school. How did it come about, in an age ostensibly dedicated to *laissez-faire* and the supreme value of individual liberty, that a change was made which severely curtailed that liberty, and in such a way as to affect not only all the children in the country, but indirectly their parents as well?

The Elementary Education Act of 1870, vital as it was, does not provide the clue to the origin of compulsory school attendance. This is rather to be sought in the Factory Acts passed earlier in the century, many of which contained clauses relating to compulsory education.[6] It is true that these educational clauses applied only to limited categories of children and were often ineffective in practice, but their very existence tells us much about the original rationale behind the policy of compulsion. They were included mainly for moral and humanitarian reasons. The moral aspect was particularly pronounced: as early as 1836 Lord Shaftesbury (or Ashley, as he then was) told the House of Commons, who were considering an amendment to the Factory Act of 1833, that the education of children affected by the Act was essential, since 'at the time most important for their moral and religious instruction, they were left without a chance of improvement. During the week they had no time, and on Sundays they were too much exhausted to attend any school.'[7] Closely related to this was the point that, if the children liable to be employed in factories were obliged to attend school for at least part of their time, the chance of exploitation would be to that extent reduced.

Most commentators would agree that the humanitarian work which eventually led to marked improvements in the conditions of child labour constitutes one of the greatest advances made during the nineteenth century. Yet one may certainly see the educational clauses of the Factory Acts, and indeed the introduction of compulsory elementary education on a national scale, as a means of securing social discipline, or even protection of the better-off members of society from the likely depredations of the lower orders. Robert Lowe, after accepting the extension of the franchise in 1867 as a *fait accompli*, argued that the provision of compulsory education was 'a question of self-preservation . . . a question of existence, even of the existence of our Constitution'.[8] The same kind of reasoning was frequently used during the School Board era. When the children of the poorer classes were first compelled to attend school, it was reported that they were 'a wild lot. . . . They had no conception of the meaning of an order and the teacher was obliged to drill them again and again in the simplest movements. The power of paying attention was almost wanting in them. . . . They had the fluid mind of the true barbarian and it was quite useless to attempt any species of coercion' – though, as other records show, coercion was in fact applied, and with success, for twenty or thirty years later it was remarked of similar groups of children 'how roughness of manner has been smoothed away, how readily and intelligently they can answer a question, how the half-hostile suspicion with which they regarded a stranger has disappeared; in fact, how they have become civilized'. Another observer considered that 'if it were not for her 500 elementary schools, London would be overrun by a horde of young savages'.[9]

Such considerations are not so far removed from present-day realities as we may like to suppose. In the early and chaotic days of evacuation during the Second World War, the Board of Education seemed to be speaking for many when it stated that 'it would clearly be intolerable that a substantial proportion of the school population should continue indefinitely to be deprived of education and its allied services, and should suffer the demoralization which must inevitably follow the removal of school discipline and control'.[10] And how often, when one has read an account of hooliganism among older adolescents, has the cry gone up that some form of National Service, or work-camp, would be the best remedy for such lack of discipline?

Another major theme which runs through the history of compulsory education has been the importance attached to education as a means of ensuring economic progress. It is perhaps doubtful whether the reformers who framed the early Factory Acts were primarily concerned with the value of the education received in relation to the children's efficiency as factory-workers, and certainly the widespread evasion of the educational clauses by employers indicates that the economic value of education was generally considered to be small. Possibly it was thought that the children, having learnt discipline at school, would be better adapted to routine manual work later, which was the old argument of the founders of charity schools in the early eighteenth century, many of whom claimed *inter alia* that the children who attended them would be 'self-supporting and inured to labour at the earliest possible age'.[11] This was, clearly, a somewhat negative argument – at least the children would not smash the machinery. A more positive view suggested that educated workers were definitely advantageous, even essential, to industry. An early exponent of such a view was an inspector of 1859, who was concerned about the lack of progress of education in colliery districts and thought that 'the necessity of educating the working classes becomes more evident every day. . . . It is the cause of the rising generation which I am advocating, of those who will have to manage and work deeper shafts, surrounded by greater dangers than any that have yet been reached and perhaps seen.'[12] Here was a technical change – the need to work deeper shafts – and education was seen as the remedy. But what kind of education? Would the rote-learning of the three Rs, which constituted the pabulum of much elementary education during this period, have been likely to produce more intelligent or more highly-skilled workers? More probably it was hoped that elementary education would form the basis for further instruction undertaken voluntarily, which would enable the workers to adapt to the changes necessitated by technical development.

Similar arguments were used at the time of the 1870 Act, and it is usual for historians of education to refer to the Paris Exhibition of 1867 which showed (unlike the 1851 Exhibition at the Crystal Palace) that Britain was lagging behind her Continental competitors, so that the need for universal compulsory elementary education was more fully realized. Indeed, the main reason given by W. E. Forster for introducing his Education Bill in 1870 was that 'upon the speedy provision of elementary education depends our industrial prosperity'.[13] There is, however, very little direct evidence that industry was able to make better use of workers who had received no more than compulsory elementary education (which meant the very great majority). Later in the nineteenth century the need for better technical education was widely urged, but it then tended to be in relation to secondary and higher, rather than elementary, education.

During the inter-war period the proposal to raise the school leaving age from 14 to 15 was supported at least in part by the contention that a better-educated working population was more likely to get Britain out of the economic depression from which she was suffering. The difficulty was that the industries most affected by the depression were the old-established ones, such as cotton-spinning and coal-mining, where the problems of technical change were complicated by economic factors well outside the reach of education as such. Although the trade unions were committed to raising the school leaving age to 16 on general social grounds, the desire to reduce unemployment among juveniles and the possibility of thus creating 'additional' jobs seem to have provided much of the impetus behind their demand.[14] Unfortunately, it was cheaper to pay unemployment benefit to some 14-year-olds than to provide extra school buildings for them all. The Education Act of 1918 had looked forward to the raising of the leaving age to 15, and local authorities were authorized to make by-laws enforcing that upper limit, but this part of the Act was shelved during the economic crisis of the early 1920s. In 1929 the President of the Board of Education announced that the leaving age would be raised to 15 on 1 April 1931, but the world slump put an end to the proposal. In 1936 a new Education Act included provision that 15 should become the leaving age on 1 September 1939, but the outbreak of the Second World War again prevented its implementation, which did not finally take place until 1947.

Thus it can be seen that economic need worked against, and not for, educational advance. Yet the argument about economic advantage has continued to be used, perhaps with more validity at a time of economic expansion, as, for example, in the Crowther Report of 1959, where the need to raise the leaving age to 16 was advocated partly on the grounds that 'the demand for more educated workers and for more deeply educated workers is growing at almost all levels in industry'.[15] Even if it is (and there are those who question this, taking the economy as a whole and the increasing use of automation[16]), it would certainly seem to be at least a possibility that the demand could continue to be satisfied by those undertaking advanced secondary and higher education on a voluntary basis rather than from among those compelled to undergo a further year of largely non-vocational studies – for in any discussion of the need for an extra year of education for all children the non-vocational aspect is necessarily stressed, because a wholly vocational training would not be sufficiently differentiated from the first year of normal employment.

There is another major theme which runs through the story of raising the school leaving age over the last hundred years. Even in the 1830s Shaftesbury had included in his discussion of the need for education the point that 'political reforms should always be accompanied by the moral education of the people. If not, those reforms would be misused, and would be turned to evil.'[17] This was in the period immediately following the Parliamentary reform of 1832, and a similar connection between the introduction of universal compulsory education and the 1867 Reform Act, which gave the vote to the workers in the towns, has often been noted, as, to a lesser degree, has the link between the extension of the franchise in 1918 and the Fisher Act of the same year. Lowe has been quoted (usually inaccurately) on the need to 'compel our future masters to learn their letters',[18] but again we must ask what connection there in fact may be between exercising the right to vote (and placing a cross, the ancient sign of illiteracy, on a ballot paper) and compulsory education. As with the economic argument, the connection is of a very generalized nature. Were the early recipients of compulsory education (who included females not yet given the vote) in a better position to exercise their democratic rights more responsibly? Only, one would think, if they were introduced to political and economic affairs as part of their schooling, a proposition always subject to criticism on party-political and other grounds. Certainly, any such notion was far removed from the minds of those who first introduced compulsory education. The syllabus laid down in the various Codes was a very limited one: even after the so-called 'class' and 'specific' subjects had been introduced, the basic idea remained that the main purpose of compulsory education was for the children to 'learn their letters'.

In the same way, we may argue that if political advantage is one of the principal reasons for extending compulsory education, then the need to raise the leaving age was never greater than between the wars, when, as we have seen, a number of attempts to do so were made without success. When the leaving age was finally raised to 15 after the Second World War, it was to the accompaniment of widespread demands for 'education for citizenship'. It may be argued, however, that such an education is premature if given at 15 or below, partly because children of that age have insufficient experience to appreciate the complex factors involved, and partly because the age at which the vote can be exercised has until recently been 21 and even with the lowering of the age of majority remains at 18. Although much can be done below sixth form level, many would see the late 'teens as the most appropriate time for the detailed discussion of political and economic issues and for encouraging the responsible use of the vote and the undertaking of public service on a voluntary or full-time basis.

If we consider other countries as well as our own, we can usually relate increased educational provision to technical and economic development, but not necessarily to improvements in social, political and cultural conditions. From the purely historical point of view, however, there would certainly seem to be an element of inevitability about the progressive raising of the school leaving age which we have noted in this chapter. A related point was made in the *Hadow Report* of 1926, which began with an historical survey, and concluded that 'it has been the general tendency of the national system of elementary education to throw up experiments in post-primary education. Though such experiments have again and again been curtailed or rendered difficult by legislative or administrative action, they have persistently reappeared in various forms.'[19] The *Report* instanced the growth of Higher-Grade schools in late Victorian times which was curtailed by the Cockerton Judgment, but which also showed very clearly that there was an increasing demand among working and lower middle-class parents and children for something better than could be offered by the ordinary Board schools. Similarly, the period leading to the raising of the leaving age to 14 was preceded by the growth of Central and other schools offering a more advanced type of education within the elementary-school system. In the same way, the decision to raise the leaving age to 15 was foreshadowed by the development of senior elementary schools and the growing demand for secondary education. It can therefore be shown, both historically and in a contemporary context, that, once a certain leaving age has been fixed, the number of children staying on voluntarily beyond that age gradually increases, so making it possible to consider a further advance in the compulsory minimum leaving age.

It is in this indisputed fact that the true explanation of the phenomenon discussed in this essay may well lie. There would indeed seem to be no 'logical' limit to compulsory education so long as the economy can afford to maintain an increasing proportion of the population in full-time education and so long as the recipients do not rise up in rebellion against it. The moral argument in favour of compulsion still has some force, but not, one would think, in the crude form in which it appeared to nineteenth-century writers. The economic and political arguments are still very generalized: no doubt the economy benefits in the long run, and it may also be true that a higher standard of education leads, by and large, to a more responsible use of the vote and a more informed interest in current affairs. But these considerations hardly seem to be specific enough to justify a major change in educational policy. Pleas for 'more education' make little sense unless the kind of education to be provided is specified in some detail. If it can be proved (as perhaps it can) that the education we are now offering our children is beneficial to them as individual human beings – judged, that is to say, on what one might truly call educational grounds – and, further, if it can be shown that an increasing number of parents are appreciating its value and voluntarily keeping their children on at school beyond the minimum leaving age, then there are good reasons to suppose that a further raising of the minimum leaving age will produce beneficial results and give the necessary impetus to those parents who, perhaps because of limitations in their own education, have failed to see the need for change.

And here we may continue to invoke the historical record in a more positive manner by pointing out what we may regard as the most hopeful aspect of the story of the successive stages by which the school leaving age has been raised from a mere 10 years old to the present 15 and the prospect of a further increase to 16. For, however bogus some of the arguments used in the past may have been, and however dependent they were on religious, economic and political factors not directly concerned with education at all, the educational benefits which have in fact accrued have been considerable. Thus the introduction of compulsory education led to the recognition of, and adaptation to, the very wide range of attainment among the children of the nation at large. The new situation was faced and practical solutions offered largely by teachers and administrators, it should be noted, rather than by politicians and economists. It was not long before 'Higher Tops' and 'Ex-Standard' classes were arranged for some children, and special classes for others who were handicapped either physically or mentally. Similarly, the raising of the school leaving age to 14 after the First World War made possible the reorganization of elementary education and the provision of something approaching secondary education for many children over 11 who had previously been neglected. The raising of the leaving age to 15 has certainly led to some improvements in secondary education and (of more doubtful educational value) to a striking increase in the number of children in all types of school who are now permitted and encouraged to take external examinations. When all children stay at school until at least 16, it may be that the futility of examinations for some children will lead to a reappraisal of our aims in secondary education which could eventually influence the whole system.

Whatever the benefits which have accrued in the past, however, it has to be admitted that the actual implementation of any decision to raise the school leaving age depends on chance economic and political factors which no historian can claim to predict. This was amply demonstrated during the inter-war period, as we have seen, and official policy since the Second World War has not been so very different. The raising of the school leaving age to 16 was envisaged in the 1944 Education Act. It was also strongly recommended in the *Crowther Report* (1959) and the *Newsom Report* (1963): the former recommended that the change should be made between 1966 and 1969, and the latter during the educational year 1969–70. Thereupon the Government announced its intention to raise the leaving age to 16 in 1970–1, but in 1968 the date was deferred until 1972–3. Nevertheless, considerable changes in our educational system have continued throughout the post-war period, usually unobtrusively and below the surface.

It is this interaction between external and internal forces which makes the history of education a complex but interesting study. So far as the history of raising the school leaving age over the last century is concerned, we may conclude that it shows all too often that educational advances take place for non-educational reasons and almost, one might say, by stealth.

REFERENCES

1 Reported in *The Guardian*, 9 January 1969 (a reference I owe to Miss Margaret Clague).
2 Fuller details may be found in Smith, F., *A History of Elementary Education 1760–1902*, University of London Press, 1931, ch. 9; and Gosden, P. H. J. H., *The Development of Educational Administration in England and Wales*, Oxford; Blackwell, 1966, chs. 7, 10.

The historical background

3 *Report of the Commissioners appointed to inquire into the State of Popular Education in England*, H.M.S.O., 1861, i, 225, 243.

4 Szreter, R., 'The Origins of Full-time Compulsory Education at Five', in *British Journal of Educational Studies*, xiii, 1 (November 1964), 16f.

5 This point, among others, is discussed in Bantock, G. H., *Culture, Industrialization and Education*, Routledge & Kegan Paul, 1968.

6 This subject is fully dealt with in Robson, A. H., *The Education of Children engaged in Industry in England, 1833–1876*, Kegan Paul, 1931.

7 Ibid., 40–1.

8 Quoted in Simon, B., *Studies in the History of Education, 1780–1870*, Lawrence & Wishart, 1960, 355.

9 Quoted in Lowndes, G. A. N., *The Silent Social Revolution*, Oxford University Press, 1937, 16, 19.

10 Quoted in Bernbaum, G., *Social Change and the Schools, 1918–1944*, Routledge & Kegan Paul, 1967, 100.

11 George, M. D., *London Life in the XVIIIth Century*, Kegan Paul, 1930, 259.

12 Robson, op cit., 157.

13 Maclure, J. Stuart, *Educational Documents, 1816–1963*, Chapman & Hall, 1965, 104.

14 See, for example, the interesting Presidential Address at the T.U.C. Conference in 1934 quoted in Bernbaum, op. cit., 62.

15 Ministry of Education, *15 to 18. A Report of the Central Advisory Council for Education (England)*, H.M.S.O., 1959, 132.

16 Bantock, G. H., *Education in an Industrial Society*, Faber & Faber, 1963, 204f.

17 Quoted in Robson, op. cit., 41.

18 Lowe did not say that we 'must educate our masters'. For the full and correct quotation, see Simon, op. cit., 355. Forster made the same point in 1870: 'now that we have given them [the people] political power we must not wait any longer to give them education' (Maclure, op. cit., 105).

19 Board of Education, *The Education of the Adolescent. Report of the Consultative Committee*, H.M.S.O., 1927, 34–5.

2 Some sociological considerations

S. J. Eggleston

One of the recurring phenomena of full-time schooling is its end. Children leave school and students leave college. One of the most illuminating opportunities to view our educational system occurs on the few days in the calendar on which leaving is permitted. On such a day the age-cohorts divide into groups. On the one hand are those who are to continue their education and retain or extend a range of life-chances. On the other hand there are those who have reached a terminal point in their full-time education and, usually, a terminal point in their life-chances. It is a moment that has been savoured in the fiction of education from Hughes' *Tom Brown's Schooldays* to Snow's *Time of Hope*. It is also a moment that has provided a focal point of educational legislation since 1870. More recently its importance has been recognized in the recent British Sociological Association study, *Comparability in Social Research*, which concludes: 'the most significant educational variable is one which combines terminal educational age with "staying on".' (Weinberg, 1969).

As with most of our educational opportunities – small classes, sixth-form studies and higher education, to name but a few – the opportunity to stay longer at school has been assumed to be in restricted supply. For all but the few the minimum school leaving age has marked the maximum extent of full-time education. Though social, economic and humanitarian arguments justifying the prolongation of full-time education in modern industrial societies have long been accepted, the provision of extended education for the masses has, until recent years, always awaited a long-delayed process of legislation to raise the minimum age of school leaving. The timing and rationale of such legislation is discussed elsewhere; all that need be said here is that in the past it has always been based on the assumption that, whatever the case in favour of the extension of schooling may be, the majority of pupils and their parents could not be expected to respond to it voluntarily. Compulsion was seen to be the only instrument appropriate to retain the vast majority of young people in the school system. As a corollary, provision for extended education had to wait upon legislation; only very rarely did it precede it. Even though each successive raising of the school leaving age moved longer education from a minority to a mass experience, it still remained that the decisions about extended education – indeed, about education generally – were exercised by a minority. The very argument of the 1944 Act (of which the 1948 raising of the school leaving age was a part) was still couched in terms of decision *for* pupils and parents rather than *by* pupils and parents.

Yet in the twenty years that have followed 1948 there have been unprecedented changes in the degree of participation in educational decisions by parents and their children that can be seen most clearly in the decisions made on the duration of schooling. In the 1950s and 1960s the watershed between compulsion and voluntarism has been crossed. To use the concepts of Turner (1961), there has been a shift from a situation in which children were *sponsored* – or not sponsored – for extended schooling towards a situation that in many ways is a more open *contest* (though sponsorship arising from the class system may still take many forms).

The changes that have taken place can best be seen by reference to the statistics. The figures have been striking, and such epithets as the 'explosion in demand' or the 'voluntary raising of the school leaving age' have been used to describe them. They marked the beginning of a challenge to the assumptions of restrictive opportunity for extended education. In 1954 the figure for pupils electing to stay on in maintained secondary schools after the minimum school leaving age was 26·1%; in 1963 after an unbroken rise it was 40·2%. But in the secondary modern schools, charged with the old senior elementary traditions of providing an education terminating at minimum leaving age for pupils who were judged to be unlikely to profit from a longer one, the rise in the same period was from 5·7% to 20·7%. After 1963 the comparison is less clear because of secondary school reorganization and the reduction in the number of school leaving dates. But by 1967 the percentage of all pupils electing to stay on in all secondary schools after the minimum school leaving age had risen to 46·6% – an increase of 17·3% over the adjusted figures for the 1957 rate. For pupils aged 16 and over the growth is relatively faster – 15% to 26·5% in the period 1957–66; for 17-year-olds it was 7·8% to 13·7% in the period 1957–65 (in all these comparisons the absolute changes in the relevant age-cohorts must be taken into account. In 1955 there were 481,000 13-year-olds in maintained schools, 755,000 in 1961 and 591,000 in 1965). At all times figures for girls run slightly behind those for boys – but the trend for both sexes is similar. There are, of course, regional variations – a generally high incidence of staying on in the south-east of England and a smaller incidence in the north-east. Within regions the range can be great. In some areas – notably those with established comprehensive schools – the staying-on rate can be almost 100% of the total population; in other areas staying on is still a prerogative of the grammar school pupil and even in those schools it may still be somewhat short of 100%.

In the light of these changes the legislation to raise the school leaving age in 1971 is likely to lead to consequences that are fundamentally different in nature from those of the raising of the school leaving age of 1942. The relative numbers of children affected will be smaller; in many areas they may only be a small minority who, for a variety of reasons, have not yet responded to the trend. A number of projections of the post-1971 situation have been made in the annual volumes of *Statistics of Education*. A particular problem in making such projections is the likelihood of 'secondary effects', both on pupils who would have stayed on voluntarily and by those who stay on compulsorily. A number of such effects are examined by Armitage, Smith and Alper (1969), who indicate some of the wide range of possible outcomes.

In many ways they will be sharply different from their fellow pupils, as the Schools Council Report, *Young School Leavers* (1969), demonstrates. Their attitudes to school and its objectives, their choice and evaluation of subjects, their acceptability of school behaviour are all significantly different. Their perception of the work and life of the school is likely, in many cases, to have made their experience of schooling fundamentally different from that of the children who stay on voluntarily. Some of them will find themselves staying on in schools and colleges that have already made extensive provision for voluntary staying on and where the pattern of curriculum, teaching method and staff/pupil relationships may have already undergone changes in response to this older group of pupils. As a result of the work of the Schools Council, local education authorities and other agencies, many will be attending schools where plans will have been made in advance in order to accommodate them – plans that received an unexpected but not entirely unwelcome extension of time as a result of the postponement of legislation in 1968.

If we are to try to anticipate some of the consequences of the 1971 situation, and particularly if we are to anticipate any of the sociological factors that may arise, it will be useful to look at some of the causes of the voluntary growth in staying on and, in particular, to look at some of its consequences for the social structure and organization of the schools. In this way at least a few of the prospects for the years after 1971 may be glimpsed.

Underlining the growth in staying on have been two well-known features of the post-war educational scene. One has been the increasing awareness of the educational needs of modern industrial society – in particular, of the growing demands for educated manpower at most levels of the occupation structure. Associated with this has been the diminution of demand for young people with minimum education. The changing shape of the employment market can be seen in the educational requirements mentioned in the situations vacant columns of newspapers from *The Times* to the local weeklies. The expansion of higher and further education had to begin with an expansion in the numbers of pupils in the upper forms of the secondary schools that could not be met by the grammar schools alone. The other major feature has been the realization that ability is at least partly determined by environmental factors and the consequent easing of the restrictive assumptions about 'limited reserves of ability' that were made in the 'genetic' era. The preliminary analysis of environmental factors was one of the major achievements of sociologists in the 1950s; the changed perception of education that flowed from it may be seen clearly by contrasting the Spens Report (1938) (on which much of the thinking of the 1944 Act was based) and the Newsom Report (1963). The Spens Committee stated:

> Intellectual development during childhood appears to progress as if it were governed by a single central factor usually known as general intelligence which may broadly be described as innate all round intellectual ability. It appears to enter into everything which the child attempts to think, to say, to do, and seems on the whole to be the most important factor in determining the work in the classrooms. Our psychological

witnesses assured us that it can be measured approximately by means of intelligence tests . . . we are informed that with few exceptions it is possible to predict with some degree of accuracy the ultimate level of a child's intellectual powers.

This is in striking contrast to the verdict of the Newsom Committee, which reported:

Intellectual talent is not a fixed quantity with which we have to work but a variable that can be modified by social policy and educational approaches. . . . The results of investigation increasingly indicate that the kind of intelligence which is measured by the tests so far applied is largely an acquired characteristic. This is not to deny the existence of a basic genetic endowment; but whereas this endowment, so far, has proved impossible to isolate, other factors can be identified. Particularly significant among them are the influences of social and physical environment; and since they are susceptible to modification, they may well prove educationally more important.

The Robbins Report (1963) published immediately after the Newsom Report reiterated the message, noting that 'The numbers who are capable of benefiting from higher education are a function not only of heredity but also of a host of other influences varying with standards of educational provision, family incomes and attitudes and the education received by previous generations'. The Plowden Report (1967) takes up the same theme and relates it to the work of the primary schools.

The upsurge of expansionism and egalitarianism was first to be seen in the post-1944 grammar schools; the extent to which staying on became the norm for all but a tiny minority of their pupils has already been mentioned. But a far more striking change took place in the secondary modern schools of the 1950s. Here the pupils were not only expected to leave at minimum leaving age, but were specifically precluded from being entered for the public examinations available to grammar-school pupils – the qualifications leading to superior occupational and social prospects. The way in which heads and teachers in these schools challenged the regulations and succeeded in providing extended courses has been chronicled by Taylor (1963), who shows how increasing numbers of their pupils were able to 'contract back into the world of superior occupational prospects from which they had been excluded by the selective process at 11'. The achievement of the secondary modern schools

Some sociological considerations 25

provided an important impetus for the development of comprehensive schools. A common feature of every version of comprehensive reorganization has been the provision of more open opportunities for extended education for pupils of a wider range of abilities. These have not only included a greater breadth of courses leading to C.S.E., O and A level examinations than even the most ambitious secondary modern schools could provide, but also, in many schools, a range of extended courses for children of lesser ability. The non-examination extended course is now seen by a number of comprehensive schools to be a legitimate area of provision.

A paradoxical but predictable consequence of the expansion of opportunity for extended education was that the schools became more open to social pressures. In absolute terms, there are usually more children from all types of home backgrounds staying on in the schools, as Benn and Simon (1970) indicate. But it is also true that a far greater proportion of children from more supportive home backgrounds tend to do so. This possibility was early recognized in the Crowther Report (1958): 'To summarize – as one goes through the categories, professional and managerial, clerical and other non-manual, skilled manual and semi or unskilled manual, the proportion of premature leaving at 15 increases in that order and the proportion of children staying on at school beyond the age of 16 decreases.'

The difference between the social classes in aspired leaving ages for their children has been reported by many researchers. It has been conveniently summarized by Douglas, Ross and Simpson (1968) reporting on their survey of children born in 1947:

> The social class pattern of leaving may be summarized by saying that the upper middle-class pupils were two and a half times as likely to stay on after the minimum leaving age as the lower manual working-class pupils, four times as likely to complete the session 1961–2 and nearly six times as likely to start session 1962–3. Part of these differences is explained by the higher measured ability of the upper middle-class boys and girls, but even when groups of similar ability are compared, the upper middle-class pupils were approximately twice as likely to stay on at each age.

In recent years a number of attempts have been made to explore some of the causal factors underlying decisions of this nature. The search has focused on the attitude of parents towards schooling and its consequences. Swift, for example, makes a distinction between types of middle-class environment. His first is the traditional one which 'sees the middle-class family providing a cultured, stimulating environment which leads to a mature interest in school work, verbal facility and habits of thought which make school work easy and pleasant'. The second type is one which has none of the advantages of the first, but in which one or both parents is characterized by frustrated ambition: 'These parents value the education system for its role in social climbing; they believe (on the basis of their own experience) that ability alone is not rewarded except in so far as it is manifested in certificates; they also have a clear and accurate picture of the prestige hierarchy and their actual (as opposed to rightful) place within it'. Schools Council enquiry, *Young School Leavers* (1968), relates differences in parental attitudes with pupils' attitudes and involvement in school; Reed (1969) has established correlations between family norms and the duration of schooling. Many other writers have explored possible causal factors of this nature, including Bernstein (1965), Goldthorpe and Lockwood (1963) and Mays (1962). Ford (1969), in her study, *Social Class and the Comprehensive School*, looks at the way in which family and class values operate in the context of a comprehensive school. She suggests that comprehensive schools may allow a persistence or even an intensification of class bias in leaving decisions.

It is not only the value of the home but also of the community that may influence decisions of this nature. In a study of Leicestershire Plan schools, the present author found that in a middle-class catchment area 89% of middle-class children and 59% of manual workers' children stayed on after minimum leaving age, whereas in a working-class catchment area only 77% of middle-class children and 30% of manual workers' children did so (Eggleston, 1966). There was some evidence that the community context influenced not only the parents, but also the pupils directly. Children from the working-class area, on being faced with the possibility of extending their education by transferring to the upper school in a middle-class area, were sometimes unenthusiastic. A typical remark was 'Catch me mixing with that bunch of stuck-up snobs.' From the schools in working-class areas there was a trickle of pupils from A streams leaving at 15 who, had they been members of grammar schools, would almost certainly have stayed on until 16. But in a number of comprehensive schools where children had the opportunity for an extended education with a predominance of their own peers the proportion of children from working-class backgrounds who stayed on was markedly greater (Eggleston, 1970). It seemed that, in conditions of voluntary staying on, children needed support from the family, community or the peer group. Middle-class children appeared to be getting it from all three sources: some working-class children from the peer group or not at all. It was not that the working-class homes or community were hostile to education – rather that they were indifferent. 'Let the lad decide' was far more the maxim than the deferred gratification ethic of the middle-class area. And the working-class community certainly provided more attractive prospects of early gratification for its young.

Studies of this nature suggest that in conditions of voluntary extended education the school not only is more subject to external influences in its ability to retain its pupils and what to offer them if they stay; it also comes to be influenced by the norms and values of its own pupil community. Clearly, if they are conducive to extended education, it is likely to have a substantial influence on all the pupils, particularly those from homes and communities where norms and values are not supportive of extended schooling. This is now realized by many schools, and the issues associated with staying on are discussed in them by pupils and teachers. Indeed, one of the volumes in a school 'Discussion Series' is entitled *Staying On* (Cave, 1968).

Yet a characteristic feature of English secondary education is that the norms and values of the pupil group are not always consensual. Instead, they are divided, often sharply. On the one hand there are groups who are able to anticipate rewards, both during and beyond their schooling, and whose attitudes are normally favourable, or at least tolerant, to the values of the school. On the other hand there are those, usually identified as pupils of 'lesser ability or motivation', or, more euphemistically, as 'Newsom Children' who come to realize that they can achieve little reward and whose attitudes to the school tend to become increasingly unfavourable.

Up to the mid-1950s the conflict between these two 'subcultures' was, as we have seen, largely outside the boundaries of any one secondary school. It was neatly expressed by an earlier euphemism, 'the difference between "the grammar school tradition" and "the emergent secondary modern tradition".' But the introduction of academic and examination prospects to the secondary modern schools brought the conflict *within* many secondary modern schools, and in so doing probably intensified feelings of 'relative deprivation' (Runciman, 1966). In the schools it is usually expressed in terms of academic streaming. As Hargreaves (1967) puts it: 'Those with positive orientations towards the values of the school will tend over the four years to converge on the higher streams; and those with negative orientations will tend to converge on the lower streams. On every occasion that a boy is "promoted" or "demoted" on the basis of school examination, the greater becomes a concentration of the two opposing subcultures.' Hargreaves' study brilliantly analyses the development of the subcultures in a secondary modern school. His juxtaposition of their characteristics is illuminating:

> For boys in high streams life at school will be a pleasant and rewarding experience, since the school system confers status upon them. This status is derived from membership of a high stream, where boys are considered to be academically successful, and are granted privileges and responsibility in appointment as prefects and in their selection for school visits and holidays. The peer-group values reflect the status bestowed on such boys by the school in being consonant with teachers' values. Conformity to peer-group and school values is thus consistent and rewarding.
> In the low streams boys are deprived of status, in that they are *double failures* by their lack of ability or motivation to obtain entry to a Grammar School or to a high stream in the Modern School. The school, as we have seen, accentuates this state of failure and deprivation. The boys have achieved virtually nothing. For boys in low streams conformity to teacher expectations gives little status. We can thus regard the low-stream boys as subject to status frustration, for not only are they unable to gain any sense of equality of worth in the eyes of the school, but their occupational aspirations for their future lives in society are seriously reduced in scope. . . . Demotion to the delinquescent subculture is unlikely to encourage a boy to strive towards academic goals, since the pressures within the peer group will confirm and reinforce the anti-academic attitudes which led to demotion, and the climate within the low streams will be far from conducive to academic striving. In order to obtain promotion from a low stream, a boy must deviate from the dominant anti-academic values. . . .

In many English secondary schools the process seems to be an almost inescapable one. It is based on a number of untested assumptions – about learning methods, about the supposed homogeneity of ability or lack of ability of streamed classes,[1] about the restriction of entry to examinations and about the limited range of opportunity held to be available in continued education and in society generally. It is reinforced by the organization of rewards within the school, as Dreeben (1968) and other writers have shown. It is strengthened by the expectations of teachers: research has shown that these can have a considerable influence on a child's achievement.² Underlying all this there may be still further sets of assumptions about the need to maintain academic standards in order to preserve a limited excellence from contamination. But above all the conflict is reinforced by the pupils themselves, whose value orientations become increasingly divergent, who reinforce the segregation in school activities by an increasing separation in leisure activities, so that they eventually come to have very real fears of the prospect of demotion or promotion to an alien subculture. By the final year the lower-stream pupils have developed a status-satisfaction system of their own by establishing what Hargreaves has called the delinquescent subculture both within and outside the school. It is one that anticipates an adult role that is frowned upon by the school. In many ways they have become different people as the previously mentioned attitude surveys in *Young School Leavers* confirm. Voluntary staying on becomes a doubly unthinkable and irrelevant act as the cultural factors inside the school reinforce those in the home and community.

In such a situation the prospect for compulsory staying on appears depressing – and the possibility that many schools would find difficulty in holding their new pupils in the extra year is confirmed by the widespread fears of teachers in discussion on this matter. As Dame Muriel Stewart put it in her introduction to *Young School Leavers*: 'The raising of the age could mean little more than the extension of a struggle between pupils who feel that school has little to offer them and teachers who feel that they meet little other than boredom and resistance.' Three-quarters of the heads interviewed in the subsequent survey anticipated major problems ahead. But many of the fears and anxieties arise from the supposed inevitability of the situation. Yet the underlying message of Hargreaves and other researchers in this field is that the situation arises in large measure not from low ability or even from background, but rather from the organization of the school itself. Hargreaves presents a detailed picture of the way in which the conflict is developed within the school. If the organization of schools does indeed play such a substantial part in the course of events, then it becomes possible to envisage new patterns of school organization that may not lead to conflicts of this nature. There then becomes a real possibility that the schools can use their extra year of compulsory attendance to offer help to the category of pupils who have so conspicuously failed to receive it in the past.

There are some signs of change. Desegregation, so that pupils and their teachers are less separated into 'ability' groups, is one of the most widespread responses of the schools. In this way the isolation that reinforced the separate subcultures is lessened. Most comprehensive schools have now gone a considerable way in this direction, though comprehensive schooling is not in itself a sufficient solution to this problem, as Ford (1969) has demonstrated. De-streaming of secondary schools may be a more positive action, as this can diminish the differential expectations of pupils, teachers and parents. Recent figures suggest that some 25% of all comprehensive schools are either totally unstreamed or unstreamed in some of their subjects (Pedley, 1969). This in itself can be seen as part of a larger movement to postpone critical selection to higher education or at least until the sixth form. But perhaps the most notable changes are those arising from a wider availability of successful achievement and a reduction of demonstrations of failure. The realization that achievement and understanding can take many forms and that the 'failure label' is often applied in a premature or even self-predicting way has been widely recognized since the National Service Survey undertaken by the Crowther Committee. It is based, too, upon a realization that success or failure may be a more adequately educative experience to the individual if he experiences it in relation to his own previous efforts rather than in relation to the efforts of his peers.

Taylor (1968) has juxtaposed two examples from the classroom that make the point well. The first is from Henry:

> Boris had trouble reducing 12 over 16 to lesser terms and could only get as far as 6 over 8. The teacher asked him quietly if that was as far as he could reduce it. She suggested he 'think'. Much heaving up and down and waving of hands by the other children, all frantic to correct him. Boris pretty unhappy, probably mentally paralysed. The teacher, quiet, patient, ignores the others and concentrates with look and voice on Boris. She says, 'Is there a bigger number than two you can divide into the two parts of the fraction?' After a minute or two she becomes more urgent, but there is no response from Boris. She then turns to the class and says, 'Well, who can tell Boris what the number is?' A forest of hands appears, and the teacher calls Peggy. Peggy says that four may be divided into the numerator and the denominator.

The second is from Holt:

> I asked Andy to make five piles of white rods, with eight in each pile; any small object would have done as well. Then I gave him eight paper cups, and asked him to divide the white rods evenly among the cups. A child who understood multiplication would have known right away that five rods were needed for each cup. A somewhat less able child might have said: '$5 \times 8 = 40$; I have forty rods; if I divide them up among eight cups I will have five rods in each cup.' Andy did neither. He started by trying to put eight rods in each cup, and ran out of rods and said, 'That won't work.' Then he put four rods in each cup, which gave him eight rods left over. I thought he would distribute these among the eight cups; to my amazement, he emptied all the cups and started all over. Then he tried to put six rods in each cup; not enough rods. Then he tried five rods per cup, which worked.
>
> One of the beauties of this kind of work is that Andy had no idea, as he struggled towards the solution, that he was making mistakes. In his clumsy way he was doing a piece of research, and without having to be told that it was so, he saw that every unsuccessful attempt brought him closer to the answer he sought. What was for a ten-year-old a very poor piece of mathematical work gave him no feeling of failure or shame, but instead a lively satisfaction, something he rarely gets in school.

Approaches based on thinking of this nature are already appearing in the secondary school. A range of curriculum research and development projects – a number of them specifically related to the raising of the school leaving age – are being developed by such bodies as the Schools Council and the Nuffield Foundation. Their approaches are being reinforced by a realization that, for young people still at school, the key requirements of adult life will more and more be the ability not to remember facts or skills, but rather to be inventive and adaptable. They are being educated for an age in which the distinctive human contribution may no longer be the capacity to recall or reproduce existing knowledge and processes. These activities are likely to have been relegated to data-storage systems and computerized automated processes. The individual's task is likely to lie largely in the capacity to adapt, develop, diagnose and respond to new situations, whether he be manager or mechanic, housewife or office worker. In consequence, an important element of most new teaching methods in secondary schools is believed to lie in individualized problem-solving approaches. Discussion of these new techniques in teaching is discussed elsewhere in this volume. But here it is important to mention the changed relationships that such approaches may bring between teacher and pupil. The teacher is likely to find himself in a new kind of partnership with other teachers and the children. No longer may he have the authority of knowing 'the right answer' in advance or even of being able to plan all the detailed stages of the learning experience. Bernstein (1967) has drawn attention to the de-structuring of teaching roles and has noted, 'There has been a shift from a teaching role which is, so to speak, "given" (in the sense that one steps into assigned duties) to a role that has to be achieved in relation with other teachers. It is a role which is no longer made, but has to be made.' The shift is reinforced by new student-regulated learning processes, such as programmed learning, language laboratory systems and the like. Bernstein, Elvin and Peters (1967) have pointed out that there may be important accompanying changes in the structure of the school from a 'stratified' to a 'differentiated' form. No longer may the 'ritualistic' devices of the house, the form and the athletic system be all-powerful; instead, control may come to rest far more on personal relationships, perhaps even 'therapeutic' in its nature. There are many possible implications for the school. For example, Bernstein, Elvin and Peters observe that 'Education for diversity of economic and social function in pluralistic societies often involves a strengthening of the instrumental and a weakening of the expressive culture of schools within the State system'.

It is important to bear in mind that there are organizational, professional and even societal impediments to changes of this nature that we have scarcely begun to examine. But even if such methods become workable for all teachers and for all schools, the solution to the problems of the compulsory extra year would still not be fully in sight. A major problem would remain the G.C.E. and C.S.E. examination system. It is a system that performs the differentiating function that schools are required to undertake in a society with an advanced division of labour. But it is an incomplete system because at least half of the school population is identified as a failure group without ever experiencing it. These are the pupils who are not entered – either because they are regarded as unlikely to obtain even minimal success therein, or because their entry would place the success rate of their schools at too great a risk. It is a system designed to assess school achievement and relate it to life-prospects, but one in which the learning of half the school population is not assessed. The implication for the nature of their school learning is unavoidable. If the schools believe that what they are able to offer their new 16-year-old pupils is valuable and important, then there would appear to be a case for allowing them to take part in examinations that measure the consequences of such schooling. Such a 'comprehensive' examination system would need to be capable of recording in detail a wide range of achievement expressed both verbally and non-verbally. Recent research suggests that the technicalities may be by no means insoluble (Wood and Skurnik, 1969) and a number of examining boards are already tentatively testing out relevant approaches. In the logic of both comprehensive education and extended education for all, the early alienation that follows exclusion from examinations and the courses leading to them seems, to say the least, incongruous and inappropriate.

In the long run a more fundamental solution for the schools may lie in the deferment of all major selective arrangements until the tertiary education stage is reached. But this depends on an availability of higher and further education that cannot be immediately foreseen. Meanwhile, intermediate moves in this direction, such as Q level examinations, to be taken at 17, may still further intensify the alienation process.

The developments – actual and prospective – that we have examined have raised the possibility of the emergence of conditions in which all pupils may see the school as offering a range of acceptable and legitimate activity like that which students at colleges of further education, universities and technical colleges tend to experience. Such a relationship is frankly contractual. It is not an easy one to relate to the compulsory-attendance regime that would follow the raising of the school leaving age, but it is by no means impossible to do so, as many industrial training schemes demonstrate. But it is certainly unlikely that it could incorporate the commitment to a set of school-imposed values that is still the model of many educators. Indeed, it is unlikely that the school will ever again have almost undisputed power to impose a set of school values upon its total adolescent population. Parsons (1961) and other investigators see the process of adolescent socialization in an industrial society as one which inevitably involves a growth of independent adolescent norms and values. The point is reinforced by Bernstein, Elvin and Peters:

Problems of continuity, order, boundary and ambivalence become socially active as the school moves to a differentiated form, or as stratified schools become de-ritualized. Pupils are then likely to generate their own consensual and differentiating rituals in order to assist in the development of a transitional identity. What is new is not this, but that the organizational setting of the school, its focus upon attributes of selected pupils, its emphasis upon skills, the bureaucratization of learning, the individualizing of failure, is facilitating the dominance of the informal, autonomous youth groups as the major source of shared values and sentiments. This shift from adult-imposed to the dominance of pupil-generated and regulated rituals is likely to weaken still further the transmission of the school's expressive culture.

But a separate pupil culture need not necessarily lead to total conflict; co-operation is an equal possibility. Recent experiences in higher education and the youth service have shown that 'client' groups with notably separate sets of norms and values may establish effective relationships with educational establishments that satisfy their needs both instrumental and expressive, even though they may in no way be committed to the 'official' values of such establishments. Moreover, if the schools, as a result of curriculum and organizational changes, find themselves able to provide for at least some of the needs of their new pupils after the raising of the school leaving age, they may, as a consequence, find themselves able to join with the universities and other establishments of higher education in a more fundamental appraisal of their value systems that has been possible heretofore. But, more urgently, they will be helping to ease the paradoxical situation in which those who have needed extended education most have been those least likely to get it. But if they fail – and the new senior pupils get no more than a continued experience of failure – not only will the legislative intent have failed, but also the internal organization of many secondary schools may fail too.

NOTES

1 Recent research on streaming in primary schools shows how the level of ability of streamed and unstreamed classes is associated with teachers' assumptions (Lunn, 1970).

2 In a recent experiment (Rosenthal and Jacobson, 1968) teachers were told that certain pupils chosen at random were late developers. The academic

performances of most of these children improved rapidly to the extent that one boy went from an I.Q. score of 61 to one of 106 and another from 88 to 128.

REFERENCES

Armitage, P., Smith, C., and Alper, P., *Decision Models for Educational Planning*, London: Allen Lane: The Penguin Press, 1969.
Benn, C., and Simon, B., *Half Way There*, London: McGraw-Hill, 1970.
Bernstein, B., 'A Socio-linguistic Approach to Social Learning', in Gould, J. (ed.), *Penguin Survey of Social Sciences*, Penguin Books, 1965.
Bernstein, B., 'Open Schools, Open Society', *New Society*, 14 September 1967, pp. 251-3.
Bernstein, B., Elvin, H. L., and Peters, R. S., 'Ritual in Education', *Philosophical Transactions of the Royal Society of London*, B., ccli 1966, pp. 429-36.
Cave, R. G., *Staying On*, London: Ward Lock Educational, 1968.
Crowther Report, Central Advisory Council for Education (England), *15 to 18*, H.M.S.O. 1959, Vols. 1 and 2.
Douglas, J. N., Ross, J. M., and Simpson, H. R., *All Our Future*, London: Peter Davies, 1968.
Dreeben, R., *On What is Learned in School*, Reading, Mass.: Addison-Wesley, 1968.
Eggleston, S. J., 'Going Comprehensive', *New Society*, 22 December 1966.
Eggleston, S. J., 'Some Environmental Correlates of Extended Secondary Education in England', in Swift, D. F. (ed.), *A Reader in the Sociology of Education*, London: Routledge & Kegan Paul, 1970.
Ford, J., *Social Class and the Comprehensive School*, London: Routledge & Kegan Paul, 1969.
Goldthorpe, J. H., and Lockwood, D., 'Affluence and the British Class Structure', *Sociological Review*, 1963, xi, 133-64.
Hargreaves, D. H., *Social Relations in a Secondary School*, London: Routledge & Kegan Paul, 1967.
Lunn, J. B., *Streaming in the Primary School*, Slough: National Foundation for Educational Research, 1970.
Mays, J. B., *Education and the Urban Child*, University of Liverpool Press, 1962.
Newsom Report, Central Advisory Council for Education (England), *Half Our Future*, H.M.S.O., 1963.
Parsons, T., 'The School Class as a Social System', in Halsey, A. H., Floud, J., and Anderson, C. A. (eds.) *Education, Economy and Society*, Glencoe, Ill.: Free Press, 1961, pp. 434-55.
Pedley, R., *The Comprehensive School*, London: Penguin (revised edition), 1969.
Plowden Report, Central Advisory Council for Education (England), *Children and their Primary Schools*, Vols. 1 and 2, H.M.S.O., 1967.
Reed, I., *An Analysis of Social Factors in Children's Education between 10 and 17*, unpublished M.Ed. thesis: University of Liverpool, 1969.
Robbins Report, Committee on Higher Education, *Higher Education*, Report and Appendix I, H.M.S.O., 1963.
Rosenthal, R., and Jacobson, L., *Pygmalion in the Classroom*, New York: Holt, Rinehart and Winston, 1968.

Runciman, W. G., *Relative Derivation and Social Justice*, London: Routledge & Kegan Paul, 1966.
Schools Council, *Enquiry, I: Young School Leavers*, London: H.M.S.O., 1968.
Spens Report, Consultative Committee of the Board of Education, *Secondary Education with Special Reference to Grammar and Technical High Schools*, H.M.S.O., 1938.
Swift, D. F., 'Educational Psychology, Sociology and the Environment', *British Journal of Sociology*, 1965, xvi, 334–50.
Taylor, W., *The Secondary Modern School*, Faber & Faber, 1963.
——, *Half a Million Teachers*, Bristol: Institute of Education, 1968.
Turner, R. H., 'Modes of Social Ascent through Education: Sponsored and Contest Mobility', in Halsey, A. H., Floud, J., and Anderson, C. A. (eds.), *Education, Economy and Society*, Glencoe, Ill.: Free Press, 1961, pp. 121–39.
Weinberg, A., 'Education', in Stacey, M. (ed.), *Comparability in Social Research*, London: Heinemann, 1969.
Wood, R., and Skurnik, L. S., *Item Banking*, Slough: National Foundation for Educational Research, 1969.

3 The pupils and their teachers

J. W. Tibble

This chapter is concerned with the 60% of the age-group who at present leave school at 15 and with their successors, who in 1972–3 will find themselves compelled to stay at school for a further year. What are the views and attitudes of the former concerning the schools they have attended and the schooling they have received? What are likely to be the reactions of the latter to the compulsory extra year? It is generally recognized that the likely answers to these questions will present serious problems for those responsible for coping with the first pupils of the extra year. As the Schools Council enquiry, *Young School Leavers*, puts it:

> The success or failure of raising the school leaving age will hinge on the success of the attempt to engage pupils more closely throughout their new five-year course. Put at its lowest, the raising of the age could mean little more than the extension of a struggle between pupils who feel that school has little to offer to them and teachers who feel that they meet little other than boredom and resistance. Schools are, by contrast, likely to be most successful with those pupils who are supported by their parents and whose interest, motivation and sense of relevance are captured by the work they do. The attempt to achieve this can better be undertaken if the schools have more information about the attitudes of those involved.

Some of this much-needed information the Enquiry provides, basing it on interviews with 4,618 young people in the 13-to-16 age-groups and 3,421 19-to-20-year-olds. The Enquiry also collected the views of 4,546 parents and 1,489 teachers of the pupils in the 149 random sample of schools covered by the survey. The main topics explored and reported on included school objectives as seen by all these groups, views on school subjects, the teachers' views on the problems raised by the extra year and how these might be met, relations between home and school and giving help with career choice. Part III of the Enquiry collects information about jobs and careers of 15-year-old leavers, their values, interests and leisure-time activities, their home backgrounds, and their school experience and attitudes to school.

Of special interest, for the purposes of this chapter, are some of the differences in opinion and attitudes between the various groups of young people and adults covered by the survey. One such difference concerned the main purposes of education and it divided school-leavers and their parents on the one hand from teachers on the other:

> Both 15-year-old leavers and their parents very widely saw the provision of knowledge and skills which would enable young people to obtain the best jobs and careers of which they were capable as one of the main functions that a school should undertake. Teachers, however, very generally rejected the achievement of vocational success as a major objective of education. It is evident therefore that conflict and misunderstanding may arise between the short-term viewpoint of parents and pupils who are concerned with starting work in the immediate future and the long-term objectives of teachers who see their responsibility as preparing pupils for the whole of their future lives.[1]

This divergence will be taken up again later in this chapter. It is also discussed in Chapter 5.

The Enquiry also uncovered significant differences between 15-year-old leavers and pupils staying on beyond leaving age in such matters as attitudes to school, school objectives, values, interests and home backgrounds:

> It can be seen that 15-year-old leavers differed most of all from those staying on at school in the quality of their home backgrounds, which were much less favourable for leavers; in being very much less inclined to have any intellectual or academic interests; and in being much more generally of an active than a sedentary bent and more interested in practical-

constructional activities than were the stayers. They also
showed differences from those staying on at school on a
number of other dimensions, although to a lesser degree. They
tended to come from larger families and more overcrowded
homes. On the whole they occupied their leisure time less
satisfactorily than did the stayers and more easily became
bored or gave their parents cause for anxiety. They were more
inclined than the stayers to resent school discipline, they were
less identified with and interested in school life, they considered
their subject curricula less useful and interesting and their
behaviour in school was more likely to be considered
unsatisfactory by their teachers. Even more than those staying
on they wanted their education to be concerned with preparing
them for their working life, but they were less anxious than
the stayers that it should be concentrated on improving their
career prospects. They more generally wished the school to
help them to develop as people and to make the most of
themselves and they wanted to learn things which would be
useful in everyday life.[2]

Other smaller-scale surveys of young people's attitudes to and views about the schooling they had received highlight some of the points made above. Thus in a report from the Adolescent Research Unit based on Northampton, 1966-8,[3] we find the following:

Though respondents make exceptions throughout the material,
it is evident that in the eyes of the young people surveyed a
great deal of contemporary schooling is boring, irrelevant and
punitive. Though respondents see this situation as arising in
part through the functioning of the schooling system provided
for the secondary age-range, they tend to stress that the major
source of their dissatisfaction lies in the attitudes of members
of staff.[4]

They recognize differences among their teachers and can readily describe good ones as having patience, tolerance and understanding, sharing their pupils' interests and experience, controlling without violence, relaxed, with a sense of humour. But they see the largest group of teachers as admonitory and domineering, even hostile and rejecting:

The consistent and repeated assertion of these groups is that
schooling is humiliating, particularly in early adolescence.

Teachers 'treat you like kids', 'like infants', 'like little ones' right through to the sixth form in some instances. Teachers are portrayed as being coercive, even violently so. Quite apart from the formal system of punishment (which, it should be noted, was rarely criticized and was perhaps generally approved), teachers enforced their will by a whole range of devices, ranging from shouting, blaming, nagging and teasing, 'showing you up', 'bossing you', and clamping down on rule observance through to a whole range of 'rough stuff'.

Other common subjects for unfavourable comment were lack of subject choice, morning assembly, 'ridiculous' rules, wearing of uniform and examination goals geared to vocational opportunities.

It is interesting to note that the older respondents who could compare their time at school with later experience in further education and work situations often made favourable comments on the latter compared with the former. In further education courses there was more choice, it was more likely to be relevant to work, uniformity in dress and manners was not stressed, lecturers 'thought of you differently' and did not 'class you as illiterate'. Similarly in the work situation young people felt they were more able to be themselves and be accepted by others, 'just as you are', faults and all.

These comments indicate a problem which is referred to in Chapter 5 of the *Map of Educational Research*:

> The problem of why some children in grammar schools and more in secondary modern schools want to bring their education to an early end may also be considered from the point of view of social psychology. From this point of view, it may be considered as a problem of the relative status of adolescents in different social situations. Whether the adolescent remains at school or has left school, he requires approval from those whose approval he values, and he needs their acceptance of the worthwhileness of the role he is required to play. He will be discontented if he finds humiliation rather than approval because the role of the learner at the end of school life seems less socially valued than that of a wage-earner.
>
> Whether his situation at school or his situation as wage-earner seems to him to carry a higher status may depend on what social group he looks to for approval. Obviously parents and teachers are likely to give their approval to school work. His contemporaries, however (those called by American

psychologists his 'peer' groups), are likely to give esteem rather to the situation of the wage-earner. It has been stated that one factor in creating dissatisfaction with the late years at school in the U.S.A. is the shift of the adolescents' motivation from desiring the approval of adults to that of desiring the approval of the 'peer' group.[5]

D. H. Hargreaves' study, already referred to and quoted from by Professor Eggleston in Chapter 2, investigates this problem in the setting of a particular Secondary Modern school:

> The members of the delinquescent subculture, if our contention that they are status-deprived is just, reject the system which confers this status and the values on which the status system is based. Such boys are thus forced to seek a substitute system which can confer prestige in proportion to the degree of rejection of the school's values. It is through the anti-academic rejection of the schools' values that informal status within the delinquescent group is achieved. They reject the pupil role and replace it with an autonomous and independent peer culture. Conformity thus becomes more important than in the academic subculture, where the boys are united through *individual* effort in academic competition. In the delinquescent subculture self-esteem is a *collective* product, since it can be obtained only in relation to the group as a whole – that is, through conformity to anti-academic group pressures – whereas in the academic subculture boys can develop self-esteem on the more individualistic basis of academic competence.[6]

Hargreaves thinks this also leads to admiration and premature imitation of adult roles beyond the school. He goes on to discuss the ways in which the school unwittingly acts as an agent in fostering delinquent values:

> The teacher thus becomes the principal *direct* agent by which the working-class boy is exposed to middle-class values. High-stream boys can internalize and abide by such values, since it is in the acquisition of such values that their hopes of future success are contained. For low-stream boys, however, the school simultaneously exposes them to these values and deprives them of status in these terms. It is at this point that they may begin to reject the values because they cannot succeed in them. More than this, the school provides a mechanism

through the streaming system whereby their failure is effected and institutionalized, and also provides a situation in which they can congregate together in low streams.[7]

The way the school is organized is, however, only one factor influencing the situation. Another important factor is the nature of the home and the attitudes of the parents, which predisposes the child to accept or reject the school values. In the case of a child from a middle-class home attending an independent or grammar school, it is obvious that the influence of home and school will be 'in line'; it is assumed that schooling into the late 'teens is a good thing, that, however unpalatable some of the food provided, it is in the long-term interests of the child to assimilate it. The schooling can lead to qualifications necessary for entry to desirable careers. There may, in addition, be strong positive family identifications with this kind of school or this particular school. If, however, the child lives in a working-class home, the home is much less likely to be in line with the predominantly middle-class values that the school embodies. The influence of the parents may range from approval of the school as a means of providing the child with better opportunities for advancement than the parents had to, at the other end of the scale, apathy or positive hostility. A child from an unfavourable home who does well in the eyes of the school, copes with the work of an A or B stream, promises to get adequate rewards for his effort in terms of examination results – such a child may well contain, though possibly at some cost to himself, the conflict between the values of home and school. But the majority of the children we are concerned with here, the present 15-year-old leavers, are children who are neither sufficiently encouraged and supported by the home nor adequately rewarded by the school.

As Hargreaves points out, it is important to realize that these factors, the nature of home and school, and such others as the influence of peer groups in adolescence and the attitudes and values of the teachers, are mutually reinforcing variables. A strong circular system of influences is set up with a 'positive feedback' which makes any break out from the system very difficult indeed. And this situation which already exists in most secondary modern and comprehensive schools (and to some extent in the lower forms of grammar schools) could be exacerbated if the existing delinquescent group were reinforced by the compulsory retention of their oldest members for another year.

This possibility is a threat, but it is also a challenge. Can we find some way of changing the situation? At what point in the circular reinforcing chain is it most feasible to attempt to break out? It is true that none of the factors mentioned is static; all are subject in some measure to the social changes operating in any society, and in our own more rapidly than any. Thus changes are going on in the home background and parental attitudes of working-class children which have produced a spectacular rise in the numbers of children staying on at school after 15. This will probably continue, but is relatively a slow process, and we need something quicker-acting. We can hardly expect the pupils themselves to initiate educational change, except perhaps indirectly through their dissatisfaction and rejection posing even more serious problems for schools and teachers. This leaves us with the teachers and administrators and the schools they are responsible for.

The Schools Council Enquiry produced evidence that teachers are indeed well aware of the problems they will face:

> For them the most frequently mentioned concern was how to prevent, or deal with, disciplinary problems arising because pupils were bored or resented being in school. Their anxiety was: 'How to teach children who would be rebellious about staying on – who already resent the fourth year now. They are mature children and grow up very quickly and would not want to be here.' Mentioned very frequently in relation to the boredom and discipline problem was the need to rethink their courses and to devise new teaching methods. 'I still worry about discipline. I try to make it more interesting, but pupils don't give me a chance to start. If anything is to be gained there must be a change of course.' 'There's the problem of adapting my subject to the interests of the people staying at school. Obviously I have got to change it in some way. At 16 you've got to keep them interested.'[8]

These comments highlight the nature of the problem faced by the teachers. They are aware that changes must be made, but think of these as changes in what they do, in type of course and methods of teaching, in adapting subjects to pupils' interests, in making careers' guidance more effective, rather than as fundamental changes in their definition of the nature and objectives of the educative process relevant to these pupils, with consequent changes in such areas as teacher-pupil relations and the organization of schools. As the Report comments in its last chapter:

Making the secondary course different is by no means the same as making it relevant. Nor will the relevance that teachers may strive to introduce necessarily be recognized as such by the pupils. For example, one of the ways in which the teachers in this sample hoped to make the curriculum more relevant was by bringing in new subjects or topics, and the greatest support was for topics which would enrich the lives of the pupils by developing their aesthetic awareness and by establishing a basis for leisure-time activities [p. 99, para. 158]. But in the view of the pupils those activities which relate to breadth of interest cluster conspicuously at the bottom of the ladder of important objectives [pp. 32–7, paras. 46–55]. Relevance, for the pupils, has clearly to do with the immediate or with the very nearly imminent; thus activities relating to the working life cluster at the top of the scale while the general interest activities group at the bottom. It will be remembered that the careers function of the school ranked comparatively low on the lists from teachers and heads [p. 41, para. 66].[9]

The Report goes on to define the dilemma for the teachers:

> Certainly, without involvement there will be no communication and therefore no response. Are teachers then to abandon their long-term objectives of personality development and all that this implies for standards of conduct and taste, and take over the objectives of pupils? Or will teachers keep their long-term ends, but modify the means to these ends? Or it may be that present practice often fails not because teachers' objectives are different from those of pupils, but because pupils are insufficiently aware of what it is that teachers are trying to achieve. This would be an argument for making objectives more explicit.[10]

We can agree that this is desirable, but must recognize that much more is involved than teachers explaining to pupils what they think they are aiming at. To see what is involved, we might begin by asking, 'Why has this problem of finding a satisfactory form of education for the children, referred to in the Newsom Report as *Half Our Future*, not already been solved?' It has been with us for quite a time. Raising the school leaving age does not in fact create any new problems; it does make existing problems more acute. Seeking the reasons for the existing problem might well take us back as far as 1902 and the decision to build a Secondary system on the narrow and selective basis of the Grammar School and to curb and limit the development of Elementary Education, which catered for the majority of children. Professor Eaglesham says:

> The Board under Morant was hostile to any expansion of higher elementary education. They were continually on the look-out for signs of 'overlapping' with secondary education. As we have seen, the higher elementary school minute cut back the development of higher-grade schools. The Board also, by means of regulations extending over several years, transferred the education of pupil teachers from the elementary to the secondary system. Furthermore, it curbed the activities of elementary teachers in evening-school work and technical education.[11]

It is true that on the positive side Morant also provided a new 'Code' for elementary education and this, as Professor Eaglesham comments, was to be for forty years the guiding light for the education of some 80% of our children. He goes on:

> the aim is a general one: there is to be preparation for life, but no vocational education. There is to be generalized training, with the assumption that this training will freely transfer to life outside school. There is also to be character training – particularly training in industry, respect and reverence; in short, training in followership rather than leadership training, suited to the working classes rather than the middle and upper classes. Finally, only exceptional children are to be selected and prepared for Secondary education.[12]

It could be said that the development of English education in the twentieth century down to the present day has been hampered by the problem of breaking out of the dual mould which Morant set it into at the beginning of the century. It should be noted that both moulds, the selective academic on the one hand, the down-graded, class-restricted elementary on the other, reflected social conditions and values already becoming out of date in 1902. The traditions he established made it harder for the educational system and its teachers to adapt progressively to the social and economic changes of the twentieth century. In particular, we note that the teachers of the 1960s, long after the term 'elementary' has officially disappeared, reflect closely in their view of educational objectives the goals set for the elementary schools by the Code of 1904. We also note that in the years following 1902 the training of teachers was moved out of the elementary orbit into the secondary. As C. H. Judd pointed out in 1914, the nature of the recruitment to the profession was being changed. The candidate

> is no longer a pupil teacher in the old sense of that term, selected by the headmaster because of his qualifications and immediately put in charge of some of the younger children; he is rather selected for higher academic training with a view to ultimate return to the schools after a course of training which takes him away for the time from the classroom and its duties.

The student teachers were 'preparing somewhat remotely for the profession rather than actual participants.'[13]

The consequences of this are clearly visible in the subsequent history of teacher-training, and indeed in the structure of colleges of education today. On the one hand, the students entering the college are the products of the academic specialized education provided in the grammar schools, from which most of them come. And they all continue this in college in the form of one (or at most two) main or special subject, studied for the student's 'personal and cultural' benefit and not for its professional relevance. On the other hand, as Judd pointed out, the colleges had taken over the apprenticeship function of the pupil-teacher system and placed great emphasis on practice teaching, provided at that time in a demonstration and practice school attached to the college. The emphasis on the importance of practical work *throughout the course*, the concurrent system, is still a feature of colleges of education; also we note that the main responsibility for the supervision of this practical work rests with the college staff and that usually all the staff, whatever their specialisms and teaching experience, share in this work. Thus we could say that a College of Education embodies *both* traditions, and in so far as the traditions conflict the contradictions are built into the college.

Of the two traditions influencing the teacher, there is no doubt that the academic or grammar-school tradition is the stronger, not only because of its higher prestige in the system as a whole, but because the majority of members of staff and their students will have spent the years from 11 to 18 in a grammar school: furthermore, most members of staff responsible for main or special subjects will have had their own teaching experience in grammar schools. We have to be aware, furthermore, that those who enter the teaching profession today are among the successful products of this academic tradition; they had to do well in this kind of study at school to qualify for entry; if they enter via a university course, they continue in the same tradition up to degree standard; if they enter via a college of education, at least half the course is in this mode. Its characteristics and the basic assumptions about the learning process which it embodies will have become internalized in the course of their own educational experience. It provides the model with which they are most familiar and which they will find it easiest to employ in their own work as teachers. If they are training for and obtain posts in secondary schools, it is also the model most commonly used in the schools and with evident success in those areas of the system which are accorded the highest prestige, grammar schools and the A and B streams of secondary modern schools.

What, then, are the characteristics of this academic model which provides the most successful kind of secondary and higher education that we have achieved up to date and which is at the same time so obviously inappropriate for at least half the secondary population? We note the following characteristics: (1) The teaching and learning go on in compartments labelled with the names of the various subjects of the secondary curriculum. The compartments are, as it were, hermetically sealed off from each other, by time-tabling and by the subject-specialism of the teachers. In the work programme the pupil is predominantly for the teacher not a whole person, but a potential mathematician or historian. He is rewarded and recognized for his skills in these subject fields. (2) The pupil is expected to identify with his teacher and what the teacher stands for, to accept the values embodied in the study of the subject, to be receptive, to sit at the teacher's feet, so to speak, at any rate during the lesson, to assume that the skills involved are worth acquiring. (3) Since the longer-term values of subject study are somewhat remote, adult and special concerns and only a minority of adolescents can be realistically expected to be motivated by them fully enough to carry them through the frustrations, difficulties and boredoms of intensive study, the school provides a system of shorter-term, more concrete, extrinsic goals as incentives for work: these are marks, form orders, prizes, examination results, culminating at the end of courses in G.C.E. and C.S.E. Certificate awards. The extension of these awards to ever larger numbers of pupils, and to growing numbers in schools for which at an earlier date such examination goals were not thought suitable, has been a notable development of recent years. The tendency for this kind of incentive to become an end in itself, the main purpose and objective of study both for pupils and for their teachers, is obvious.

Further extensions in the applicability of this model to larger numbers of secondary pupils are likely; the percolation of middle-class standards into working-class homes continues; the C.S.E. has extended the range of pupils to whom examination incentives can apply; the work of the Nuffield Foundation and the Schools Council provides a basis for the revision of content and methodology over the whole range of secondary subjects. But it seems clear that, at any rate in the foreseeable future, the model outlined above cannot be successfully used with the majority of the children with whom we are concerned in this book. As the surveys show, the present school-leavers at 15 do not find it easy to identify with their teachers and schools. Preoccupied with the need to discover themselves and be recognized by others as whole persons, they do not take readily to the compartmented disciplines of subject studies; long-term and general objectives in terms of good citizenship, rewarding leisure-time pursuits, worthy characters or whatever have little meaning for them. Their goals are short-term and concrete – getting a job, earning money, being approved by their fellows, having a good time while they can, watching television, playing games; any effort they put into school studies is not likely to be adequately rewarded.

If the academic model cannot be made to suit these pupils, we may ask whether there are any alternative models of the educative process which might be more suited to their needs. The answer is that such models do exist. Unfortunately for our purpose, they have been used most successfully in the education of young children in the infant and junior ranges. There are fewer examples of their successful application in the education of older children for a variety of reasons: the lower prestige of secondary modern schools and their understandable tendency to emulate the higher-prestige grammar schools and see success in terms of examination awards for their brighter pupils; the compartmented structure of these schools and the higher rewards attached to subject specialization on academic lines; the teachers' own internalization of the academic model; the relative lack of the kind of equipment and support needed by the teacher trying out experimental courses; the difficulty of validating courses and assessing their success if conventional testing and examination procedures are not relevant. There are welcome signs that the necessary guidance and support for the teacher from outside the school may be more available in the future through the extension of advisory services, the encouragement of team teaching, the provision of teachers' centres, the expansion of in-service courses and the supply of validated teaching materials from the

Schools Council and other sources. It is at any rate no longer assumed by administrators that the main and perhaps only 'aid' a teacher needs is a text-book, written by another teacher and often validated only in terms of the examination successes of the pupils using them.

But there is still a long way to go. And what needs stressing most, perhaps, at this moment is, on the part of the teacher, the different basic assumptions he must acquire if new approaches are to be successful, and, on the part of administrators, advisers and educationalists, a realization of the extent and kinds of provision, help and support the teacher will need. However, we do know what the basic characteristics of the alternative models must be, even if we do not yet know enough about how to apply them to meet the needs of older children and especially of those in the 13-to-16 age-range. First, the teacher does not assume that his pupils will be able to identify with him and be able to understand or at any rate accept what he is up to. He is prepared to start where his pupils are, in a sense to identify with them, to understand them in their present reality (which may include large elements of what to him seems fantasy). It is encouraging, at least, that in the case of young children, their teachers, despite the dominance of the other model in their own education, can be trained to acquire the necessary skills and apply them with reasonable success. I do not think the skills involved in adapting this model for use with older children are essentially different; but they may be more difficult to acquire. This is partly because of the strength of the reinforcing variables referred to earlier, operating in both the school organization and in the teacher himself. In listening to a disgruntled or rebellious adolescent, accepting the validity of his feelings and opinions (though not necessarily agreeing with or justifying them), the teacher may feel his is working against the grain of the system, letting down his colleagues, weakening authority. But it is partly also that a rebellious 16-year-old is a more serious threat in reality than a young child in a temper tantrum. The fear of disciplinary problems looms large in the mind of the student in training, as it did indeed for many of the teachers in the survey contemplating the extra year. Secondly, it must be realized that starting where the young person is, listening, encouraging discussion, not being shocked, taking what is there – all this is only the starting-point. The teacher has then to use his understanding of the pupil and the relationship he has built up with him to promote learning of something he has judged the pupil is capable of and can be induced to co-operate in. The point is, he has not come with a ready-made programme, a syllabus, which the pupil has to accept; he is prepared to work out a programme with a pupil or group of pupils which meets both their wishes and his; it is his responsibility to see that some worthwhile learning (in his judgment) ensues; his skill lies in convincing them that this is not incompatible with their present interests or short-term future needs. In this way of working one could say that the syllabus is what they produce at the end of the course, not what they start with. Thirdly, in this model, the incentives are intrinsic to the task and arise from the acceptance by the pupil of its value and relevance. The conventional examination incentives are in any case inappropriate for the majority of these young people. But this does not mean that the assessment and evaluation of the work are not important. The learner should, however, participate in the evaluation, so that he leaves school with some capacity for self-evaluation. One could in any case criticize the academic model because it leaves evaluation and assessment to the teacher and excludes the pupil from it, to the exaggerated extent in formal examinations of not letting him know the results in detail and making no use of the finished product. As has been pointed out many times, to understand the intricacies and rituals of examination procedures, we have to think of them as the counterparts in our society of initiation rites in more primitive societies. If there is to be the transfer from skills learned in school to life after school, it is essential that evaluatory procedures be built into the learning process and acquired by the pupils, with, of course, the teacher's guidance.

I am suggesting then that if the new kinds of courses envisaged by teachers questioned for the Survey (and now being developed, for example, in the Schools Council Humanities Project) are to be successful, some drastic changes in teacher assumptions and attitudes to the work are required. In particular, this involves a change in the relationship between teacher and learner from that provided by the academic model. There must be more reciprocity in the relationship. Teachers must demonstrate that they are learners too, and can learn with and at times from their pupils. They must get across more effectively to young people that they *believe* in education as an ongoing and lifelong necessity in a rapidly changing society. And they must not limit these pupils' achievements, as happens frequently in the academic model, by streaming and typing them. Some recent research has demonstrated how much the teachers' assumptions about the pupils and his grading of them can in fact condition their performance: or at any rate his assessment of it.

The importance of the connection between curriculum and teacher/pupil relations was the theme of a talk by Derek Morrell, given a few months before his untimely and lamented death in December 1969:

> To understand what is really going on in school, we have to come to grips with extremely complex, constantly changing and immensely particular systems of person interaction, involving complex relationships between the experience, language and values which the pupils bring into the school from their homes and neighbourhoods, and those which are imported by the teacher.
>
> In a nutshell, if there is positive reciprocity of feeling and aspiration as between the teachers and the taught, satisfying to both, there is a describable curricular reality: the teachers are contributing to the learning which is taking place, they are helping to create new realities. But if there is no such reciprocity, if there is a total absence of mutual emotional satisfaction, the curriculum remains simply an idea in the minds of the teachers: it lacks reality, even though the teachers teach and the children go through the motions of scholastic activity. . . .
>
> My point is rather that it is a waste of time to fuss about what we think the children should learn if we do not understand how to organize a system of pupil-teacher relationships which is productive of our intended learnings. And cognitive development is not something apart from growth towards emotional maturity: it is both the tool and the product of such growth. To live is to feel. To know and to think is to acquire the ability to select those responses to environmental pressures and opportunities which will maximize a feeling of well-being, or happiness – which is the result of maintaining a secure identity within a constantly changing and often threatening relational system.
>
> The object of the exercise is to help children towards an integrity of two rationalities – that of feeling, which is no less real than cognitive rationality, but which may be largely private to the individual child, reflecting his experience of a hostile, unloving world: and that of cognitive rationality, which has to be painfully built by the careful, disciplined analysis of all available experience, and which then provides a means of sharing our feelings with others, maximizing those

which are productive of reciprocal satisfaction, and minimizing those which shut us up in a hostile private world. . . .

But at worst a teacher whose criterion of success is academic achievement finds himself confronted with young adolescents who, as they emerge from the emotionally dependent world of childhood, can see no realistic possibility of achieving a satisfying adult identity by surmounting the hurdles erected by a meritocratic society – whether because they reject the values of that society, as represented by the teacher, or because (not being fools) they are beginning to realize their own limitations, or because they are beginning to find that other learning situations, external to the school, are more rewarding.

There is then no possibility of reciprocity of feeling or aspiration, and opting out occurs, as it is bound to do unless the teacher is responsive to the feelings and aspirations of the pupils and adjusts his own position – if society will permit him to do so – in order to create or re-create a positive reciprocity of relationships.[14]

Those who are going to be concerned with the education of young people compelled to stay on for the extra year could hardly do better, in my view, than take the mature insight of Morrell's last testament as a guide.

REFERENCES

1 *Young School Leavers*, H.M.S.O., p. 45.
2 Ibid., p. 221. See also Figs. 16 and 17 for a graphic presentation of these differences.
3 Richer, R. L., 'Schooling and the Self-concept', *The New Era*, 49, No. 7, July/August 1968. The survey used open-structured interviews in the setting of youth clubs, involving forty clubs and 590 interviewees.
4 Ibid., p.187.
5 Thonless, R. H., 'Adolescent Attitudes towards the Educational Process', in *Map of Educational Research*, N.F.E.R., pp. 62–3.
6 Hargreaves, David H., *Social Relations in a Secondary School*, Routledge & Kegan Paul, p. 172.
7 Ibid., p. 174.
8 *Young School Leavers*, p. 86.
9 Ibid., pp. 241–2.

10 Ibid., p. 242.
11 Eaglesham, E. J. R., *The Foundations of 20th-Century Education in England*, Routledge & Kegan Paul, pp. 51–2.
12 Ibid., pp. 53–4.
13 Judd, C. H., *The Training of Teachers in England, Scotland and Germany*, 1914.
14 'Happiness is not a Meal Ticket', *The Times Educational Supplement*, 19 December 1969.

4   Economic aspects

John Sheehan

Some of the economic aspects of the extra year of compulsory education were highlighted when the measure was postponed for two years in January 1968 as part of the Government's crisis measures following on the devaluation of sterling in November 1967. These related to its effects on public expenditure, and the savings due to postponement were estimated by the January 1968 White Paper, *Public Expenditure in 1968–9 and 1969–70*, at £33 million in both 1968–9 and 1969–70. These savings were principally in the form of reductions in the school-building programme previously scheduled for these financial years. This, however, is an incomplete and short-term view of the economic issues involved; the full economic implications are wider and often more difficult to identify.

It is incomplete because the White Paper (like other official publications) was concerned only with the implications for public expenditure. This expenditure, which measures resources paid for by the public authorities and used in education, does not necessarily measure its real or economic cost. There is also the question of the pupils who are being educated, and the extent to which an extra year of full-time formal education deprives the economy of potential members of the labour force, thereby lowering national output. Also the savings mentioned above are merely temporary, as they represent the postponement of capital expenditure. More important in the long term is the commitment to extra recurrent expenditure which the raising of the school leaving age involves. There are further aspects which are much more difficult to analyse. For

Economic aspects 55

example, what will be the indirect or secondary effects of the extra year, i.e. will it accelerate the existing trend towards increased 'staying on' after the compulsory leaving age and thus lead to an even greater demand for higher and further education? There are economic benefits as well as costs, which may assume significance after a considerable period. Will the formation of skills be aided, as well as the technical training demanded by a growing economy and by technical change? How much will the extra year contribute to the growth of the economy through its effects on the stock of human resources? Some of these questions, it will be seen, cannot be answered fully.

The Financial Impact

What is the additional financial commitment entailed by raising the school leaving age to 16 in the academic year 1972–3? The first item to be considered is the capital cost, i.e. the cost of constructing the extra schools, classrooms and other facilities demanded by the extra pupils. According to an announcement by the Secretary of State for Education and Science made in January 1969, the cost of the revised special building programme planned in connection with the change would be £25m. in 1970–1, £35m. in 1971–2 and £45m. in 1972–3, a total of £105m. over the three years. The size of this building programme may be compared with that of the normal capital expenditure on replacement, expansion and improvement of maintained schools. These expenditures may fluctuate from year to year, so that annual comparisons are not necessarily meaningful; but for the three-year period of 1970–3 the special building programme accounts for nearly a quarter of all capital expenditure on maintained schools.

The postponement of the extra year and of the special school-building programme for two years yields a saving in capital expenditure of £33m. in 1968–9 and £48m. in 1969–70, according to the Prime Minister's statement of 16 January 1968. It is not clear exactly what impact the postponement will have on capital expenditure in the financial year 1970–1 (the final year of the original building programme and the first year of the revised programme) as the phasing of the two programmes appears to differ with the bulk of expenditures now falling in the later years. It is thus likely that there will be a small saving in 1970–1.

To summarize, the postponement of the raising of the school leaving age will mean that the bulk of the necessary capital expenditure (about £80m.) will be transferred from 1968–70 to 1971–3. This is broadly in accordance with the Government's post-devaluation policy of restraining the growth of public expenditure, which, according to the January 1968 White Paper, is expected to be 2·8% per annum in real terms during the period 1967–8 to 1969–70. The latest indicators (from the Chancellor's Budget speech of 15 April 1969) are that this target is being achieved, although other economic trends – which in the long term must have an influence on the resources available for education – may not be entirely in accordance with expectations. The figures given above have related the capital cost to capital expenditure on maintained primary and secondary schools. Capital expenditure on all types of education in England and Wales (including further and higher education) amounted to £227m. in 1966–7, and consequently the extra capital expenditure is about 15 per cent of total educational investment, or less if the latter figure follows its previously rapidly rising trend, which seems likely, despite the Government's austerity measures.

A calculation of the amortisation costs (or 'loan charges') arising from capital expenditure is necessary if capital and current costs are to be added. To calculate the loan charges arising from capital expenditure, it is usual in local education authority practice to assume that buildings are amortised over a sixty-year period. The rate of interest should equal the cost of long-term borrowing to the Government. Currently this is almost 9% per annum, but this rate could well be exceptional, due to the present financial situation. Nevertheless, it is realistic to assume quite a high rate, and we have chosen 8%. In that case the extra capital charges amount to about £9m. per annum. This represents (very approximately) the annual flow of services rendered by the £105m. worth of extra school buildings.

The current expenditure implied by the extra year is considerably larger (especially in the long run) than capital spending. It is also more difficult to calculate – and the difficulty increases with the length of time for which forecasts are made. The forecasts below are confined to the first year – 1972–3 – and some general remarks are made about cost trends in subsequent years. In order to calculate current costs, some projections and forecasts of extra enrolments and costs per pupil must be made.

In March 1969 the Department of Education and Science estimated that 287,000 extra pupils were likely to be in school in 1972–3 as a result of the change.[1] This may be contrasted with the 350,000

Economic aspects 57

extra expected when 1970–1 was the target year. The difference is largely due to the trend towards increased 'staying on' in school after the school leaving age, which has been quite marked in recent years, as the following figures show:

Percentage of 15-year-old age-cohort in maintained schools

Year (January)	Percentage
1963	36·1
1964	51·3
1965	52·8
1966	54·6
1967	56·8
1968	59·8

Source: *Education and Science in 1968*, Cmnd. 3950, p. 29.

The large increase in the enrolment ratio between 1963 and 1964 is a result of the Education Act of 1962, which was the last extension of the school leaving age, and as a result of which 15-year-olds were no longer permitted to leave school at the end of the Christmas term. There has been a steady (and strictly 'voluntary') increase in the ratio in all subsequent years, with the result that the proportion of 15-year-olds at school rose from 36% in 1963 to almost 60% in 1968. The proposed extra year will raise this ratio from 60% to 90% during the subsequent five-year period from 1968 to 1973.[2] Thus the proposed extra year of schooling has been anticipated to a considerable extent by these trends (which are expected to continue until 1972–3) and its impact thereby lessened. The rise in absolute numbers enrolled has not been as large as these percentages suggest, because of demographic factors; but the trends have nevertheless helped the proposed change, as a sudden large increase in enrolments poses administrative, financial, economic and educational problems for the educational system.[3] The administrative problems are evident, and the financial problems are indicated by the cost estimates made here. The economic and educational problems arise from the fact that it is difficult, if not impossible, to arrange a sudden increase in resources of buildings and teachers to match a sudden increase in enrolments. Either these resources are built up in advance, in which case under-utilization will probably occur, or they may lag, in which case overcrowding and a deterioration in staffing standards will presumably lead to deleterious educational results.

The extra recurring expenditure in the years following 1972–3 becomes more difficult to calculate because of the presumed continuing tendency towards an increased proportion of voluntary enrolment, even though the 15-year-old age-cohort will increase by an average of about 25,000 per annum between 1973 and 1978. But as enrolment will in fact be compulsory, one cannot calculate the voluntary element; one can merely infer it from previous trends. Thus the real or opportunity cost of increasing the school leaving age becomes more and more a matter of guesswork from 1974 onwards.[4] Consequently, current costs will be calculated for 1972–3 only; at present this involves making projections of voluntary enrolment trends for a five-year period, which are open to error and criticism.[5] But at least these figures can be checked against future data, whereas post-1972–3 figures cannot be, and the amount of projection involved is the minimum necessary to derive a cost estimate for the first year. The reorganization of secondary education on comprehensive lines may also be a complicating factor, which we will not pursue further.

As with the capital-cost estimates, constant prices will be used, i.e. we will abstract from any cost increases due purely to inflation. Even so, the estimation procedure is complex and contains many pitfalls. The assumptions which underlie it should be carefully noted. Basically, these derive from the fact that national income *per capita* will influence current costs, because these costs are largely composed of the salaries of teachers and other personnel. 1966 prices are used, as 1966 is the latest year for which comprehensive and reliable data are available.

Basically the cost projections were made by projecting 1966 current direct costs per pupil to 1972–3, allowing for the influence of the growth of national income on unit costs. A further adjustment was made for expected changes in the pupil-teacher ratio. The result was that direct costs per pupil in 1972–3 were estimated at £137·5, and total current costs per pupil at £167·5. For the 287,000 extra pupils this gives a total current cost of £48·5m. in 1972–3, composed of £39·5m. direct expenditure and (approximately) £9·0 loan charges.[6]

The financial costs can at this stage be compared to total educational expenditure, total Government expenditure and the gross national product. Official forecasts of educational and Government expenditure exist only as far ahead as 1969–70, and at 1967 prices.[7] Adjusting to 1966 prices, and allowing a growth rate of 3% per annum in real terms (in line with current Government policy) for

Government spending and 2% for the gross national product (broadly consistent with assumptions made above), the 1972-3 figures are £16,755m. and £35,820m. for Government spending and national product respectively. On similar assumptions, the total of educational spending (capital and current) should be £2,365m. Total costs of raising the school leaving age will be, by comparison, £93m. in 1972-3. But this is an unusually high figure, as it includes an exceptional amount of capital expenditure. A more representative figure (current expenditure plus loan charges) is £48·5m., which amounts to 2·1% of total educational expenditure, 0·29% of total Government expenditure and 0·14% of national expenditure or the gross national product.

The Full Economic Cost

Any comprehensive cost calculation should at least estimate the important cost entailed in transferring some of the potentially active labour force to 'non-productive' activities – in this case to full-time education. This is equivalent to the production or output of goods and services lost by such a transfer (in economic terminology, the 'opportunity cost' of transferring labour from one activity to another), and is usually measured by the incomes foregone by the workers concerned. There are, however, some objections to the economic theory underlying opportunity cost calculations of this type.

Firstly, the general proposition that wage equals marginal product (i.e. the product of the last worker taken into employment) may be contested. This proposition rests on the assumption that labour markets are perfect, i.e. that there are many buyers and sellers, none of which is powerful enough to influence market forces, that these all have perfect knowledge of market conditions, and that there are no institutional barriers or constraints to their behaviour. Such a scheme of things is far removed from reality, however. Trade unions, large employers or groups of employers, lack of labour mobility, lack of knowledge – all tend to make markets imperfect (in this context 'imperfect' should not be understood as implying disapproval, but merely as constituting a departure from certain assumptions of economic theory), and thus tend to weaken any necessary connection between marginal product and wage.

Secondly, in the case of the 287,000 15-year-olds special difficulties arise. Their wages may be fixed according to certain differentials from other, older, workers. Alternatively, earnings of young people, especially those in apprenticeships, may be less than their productivity, because of the value of the training they receive.[8] Finally, the size of the group may be more than 'marginal' in relation to the labour force, and therefore present earnings data may not serve as an adequate guide to its productivity.

These theoretical points merely indicate trends in the relation between wages – especially the wages of young people – and productivity. They do not tell us anything about the exact nature of these relationships, but are useful as a warning that the estimate given below is to be regarded merely as an approximation – apart altogether from the various statistical difficulties and assumptions which will be encountered.

In 1967 average weekly earnings for juvenile manual workers were 199/6d (males) and 138/10d (females). This relates to manual workers, whereas what is really needed is information relating to the 287,000 who will be compelled to stay at school in 1972–3. However, most indications are that there is a strong association between voluntary 'staying-on' at school and social class,[9] and that manual workers and their children, who receive the least amount of education, should be the great majority of the 287,000 in question. Consequently, the earnings statistics for manual workers (the only readily available juvenile earnings statistics) should be taken as being representative. The available information relates to males under 21 and females under 18, and consequently probably overstates the earnings of 15-year-olds. On the other hand, the fact that actual earnings of the relevant 15-year-olds may understate their productivity for reasons given earlier would tend to offset this.

Using these earnings data as a basis, and making the same assumptions as in the previous cost projections (namely, constant prices, a 2% growth rate per annum in income per head, and no change in *relative* earnings) we get a figure of 224/8d per week for males and 156/3d for females in 1973. Of the 287,000 pupils, approximately 51% are males and 49% females,[10] and applying a weighted average of earnings foregone, a total figure of £142·4m. per year is arrived at. This may be taken as an approximate indicator of the cost of the extra year represented by withdrawals from the labour force, or reduction in output. It is approximate because no allowance is made for unemployment; the true figure is probably 10% or 20% lower. It should be regarded as a short-term estimate only; in the long run there are various other effects, some in the form of economic returns which may be important, and which could outweigh any short-run costs. It is to these broader, long-term issues we now turn.

Some Long-term Aspects

Two major economic arguments are usually given in favour of a high level of education (and thus, by implication, in favour of raising the school leaving age). These are: (*a*) that a high level of education is necessary to meet the manpower needs of a highly developed economy and (*b*) that education leads to a higher rate of economic growth or leads to higher incomes. These arguments, it will be seen, are interconnected. Also the question of the link between education and economic growth may be distinguished from the link between education and higher incomes (i.e. the rate of return to education); the latter could be positive for individuals even if there were no economic growth. Before we examine these questions, an important clarification is needed. Many educators and others would object to attempts to justify education or more education on economic grounds for the reason that there are more important criteria for the provision of education, and more fundamental values involved. And, of course, they are right, or almost right. There are more important criteria, and the policy-maker is well advised to remember this. But even where a decision on educational policy is taken on social, political or some other non-economic grounds, it will inevitably have economic effects. Even though economic aspects of certain decisions do not determine policy, it can hardly be useful in any way to be ignorant of them; furthermore, in a case which is marginal from the social or political point of view, economic aspects may be a useful guide to policy. As for trying to justify educational decisions on economic grounds, the important thing to remember is that these grounds should not be used alone. To say that they should not be considered at all is surely to go too far. Consequently, the economic arguments analysed here are to be seen in their proper perspective: as subordinate (ultimately) to the questions considered in other chapters, but none the less of interest in themselves, and of use in certain areas of policy-making where other criteria are not directly involved, or do not give any particular guidance.

The link between education, manpower needs and economic development has been put forward as a criterion for educational expansion and improvement, and has resulted in actual educational development plans in some countries. It is not merely an argument for certain kinds of technical education; it is also held that general education is in many respects a prerequisite for the achievement of certain occupations and skills. This line of study and planning has been associated in recent years with the Organization for Economic Co-operation and Development (O.E.C.D.), and especially with the various documents and reports published in connection with the O.E.C.D. Mediterranean Regional Project and Educational Investment and Planning Programme. It is argued that for technical progress and economic growth there is a need for a large proportion of highly qualified and specialized manpower – especially scientific and technical manpower – in the labour force. Generally, in these studies increases in the gross national product and in the output of various sectors of the economy are correlated with changes in the occupational structure of the labour force, which in almost every case indicates a higher proportion of skilled and highly trained workers as output increases. The next step is to ascertain educational qualifications or levels corresponding to or necessary for the acquisition of these skills. This gives a basis for quantifying the educational needs of the economy and for expanding and developing the educational system. These trends and needs are usually based on projections of past trends, the analysis of intentions and requirements of employers, the analysis of industrial structure, or on interfirm and international comparisons. By implication, if educational 'output' is inadequate, workers with the necessary skills will not be forthcoming in sufficient quantity (or else they may be of insufficient quality), and productivity, output and the rate of economic growth will be depressed. This is an extremely simplified description of part of the 'manpower approach' to educational planning and development. However, it emphasizes some of the relevant issues which are open to criticism.

First, the link between educational and occupational categories is by no means fixed, as the manpower requirements approach to education would seem to imply. Technological change is one important reason for this; furthermore, it is difficult, if not impossible, to forecast such change. Another reason is that some educational qualifications may lead to many possible occupations (arts graduates may become different types of executives in industry and public administration, for example). Cases such as doctors, where training is quite specific and transfers to other occupations almost nil, are quite exceptional; even for engineers and teachers there may be alternative methods of training. Similarly, the rapidly expanding system of further education in the United Kingdom is an important means of technical training, whether apart from or in conjunction with various forms of 'on-the-job' training. As far as demand for skills is concerned, it is probably more important (and certainly more flexible) than an extra year of full-time general education. This is not to deny the value of the latter; rather to point out its probable minor direct significance for manpower needs. Indirectly, of course, it may be of importance, as a good general level of education can help to make subsequent training more effective.

Second, the relation between output and occupational requirements is not known precisely, again partly because it is not a fixed relationship. Thus it becomes difficult to infer the educational requirements of economic growth. This does not necessarily deny the validity of all attempts at manpower forecasting and educational planning. It merely demonstrates that our knowledge is not sufficient to evaluate the precise effects of an extra year of general education for some of the labour force, especially in view of the opportunities available for part-time further education, apprenticeship and on-the-job training, both formal and informal, which are so important for the formation of skills. We can say that a high rate of economic growth and technical change will necessitate a high degree of flexibility in the labour force, which must be able to adopt new techniques and learn new skills, and that this process will be facilitated by a higher general level of education. The extra year should be an improvement from this point of view, provided that the quality of education is maintained for all pupils.

The other 'economic' argument for education – that it promotes economic growth – also needs to be examined in the context of the proposed extra year. This argument is conducted on two levels.

First there is the approach of Denison and others[11] who have analysed the sources of economic growth in the U.S.A. and Western Europe in recent years. The basis of their method is to measure the growth of national output on the one hand and the growth of the various inputs which produce this output on the other. The weighted average rate of growth of inputs (land, labour and capital) is found to be significantly less than the growth of output. The difference in growth rates, or 'residual', is ascribed to technical progress, research and development, and education. The educational contribution is not only contained in the 'residual' (in the form of advances in knowledge), but also in the increase in labour inputs (in the form of extra years of education embodied in the labour force). Altogether, education has been estimated to account for as much as 40% of the growth of output.

There are two main reasons why this type of analysis and the conclusions drawn from it may be questioned: (a) they depend on certain postulates of economic theory – notably the marginal productivity theory of income distribution and the aggregate production function – which would not be fully acceptable to many economists, and (b), as Jorgenson and Griliches[12] have shown, further statistical refinement of the data used may reduce the 'residual' to almost zero – and with it much of the inferred contribution of education to economic growth. This is not the place to pursue these controversies, but merely to demonstrate that such economic arguments for education are by no means as reliable as their widespread acceptance by policy-makers might indicate.

The second argument for linking education and economic development is because of the effects of education on individuals' earnings. Lifetime earnings and education show a strong positive correlation, and it can be shown that both for individuals (reckoning only costs and returns to the individual) and for the State (making a different 'social' estimate of costs and returns) there is a positive rate of return to educational 'investment', which in some cases is greater than the rate of return to physical investment.[13] Blaug[14] estimates the private rate of return on secondary and higher education in Great Britain as 14% in 1963, and the social rate as 8%. But education and ability, education and social class, education and wealth are also positively correlated, so these results lose some of their validity. Furthermore, returns derived from data relating to the past need not have any close connection with future returns, especially at a time of rapid educational expansion, such as the present. Finally, unlike a completed secondary or higher education, an extra year of compulsory full-time education does not necessarily lead to any distinct qualification or degree and its direct value for vocational purposes may not be as great. Thus, the 'rate-of-return' analysis of education does not provide a reliable guide to policy in the case of the extra year under review.

Some Conclusions

These remarks on the wider economic effects of raising the school leaving age may seem negative. This is largely because there are still serious gaps in our knowledge of education-manpower and education-economic growth relationships, so that any attempt at positive statements about economic aspects of education must take these deficiencies into account. There are, however, certain long-term trends and international comparisons which can be made from existing data, and these may help to put the proposed extra year in a better perspective. First, the level of education of the labour force in some developed countries may be compared, using data compiled by Denison for his study of U.S.A. and European economic growth, *Why Growth Rates Differ*. Unfortunately, data for the countries concerned are not available for the same year, but this defect is lessened by the fact that the composition of the labour force changes relatively slowly. The comparisons are given in the following table:

Percentage distribution of male labour force by years of education completed

Years of School Completed	United States (1957)	France (1954)	United Kingdom (1951)	Italy (1961)
0	1·4	0·3	0·2	13·7
1–4	5·7	2·4	0·2	26·1
5–6	6·3	19·2*	0·8	38·0*
7	5·8	21·1	4·0	4·2
8	17·2	27·8	27·2	8·1
9	6·3	4·6	45·1	0·7
10	7·3	4·1	8·4	0·7
11	6·0	6·5	7·3	0·6
12	26·2	5·4	2·5	1·8
13–15	8·3	5·4	2·2	3·0
16+	9·5	3·2	2·1	3·1

Source: Denison, op. cit., ch. 8.

* The French percentage relates mainly to six years of education, and the Italian to five, thus increasing the gap between Italy and the other countries.

In the United Kingdom, compulsory education has been very effective in eliminating the under-six years completed group, when compared with the U.S.A. and other countries. In the U.S.A., however, there is no sudden drop in the percentage after the group corresponding to compulsory schooling period. This is partly a result of different compulsory education requirements over the past fifty years in various states, but largely a result of a strong tendency to stay on after the compulsory leaving age. Thus in the U.S.A. the largest percentage of the labour force in any single group (26·2%) is in the twelve years completed group. The corresponding group in the United Kingdom accounts for only 2·5% of the male labour force. As the United Kingdom figures in the above table relate to 1951, the effect of the previous extension of the school leaving age (to 15) in 1945 did not have much effect. A similar table for recent years would show a large proportion in the nine- and ten-year categories, whereas in 1951 the eight- and nine-year categories (with 27·2% and 45·1% of the labour force respectively) are predominant, the percentage with ten years of education being only 8·4%, a reflection of the low rate of voluntary enrolment in the years before 1951. Also the table shows how compulsory education in the United Kingdom has been more rigorously enforced than in France and Italy, and at a higher age.

Another international comparison made by Denison for the year 1957–8 shows the average number of years of education given to 'completed' students. For the United Kingdom this is comparatively high, but it is a function of the low starting age rather than any tendency to stay at school after the compulsory leaving age. Thus, the average starting age in the U.S.A. was at 6·1 years, the average leaving age 19·0 years, and average years of education 12·9. For seven north-west European countries – Belgium, Denmark, France, Germany, Netherlands, Norway and the United Kingdom – the overall average starting age was 5·9, leaving age 16·2, giving 10·3 years of education. For the United Kingdom, the figures are 5·1 years, 16·1 years and 11·0 years respectively. Thus in the United Kingdom, even though students received more years of education than in north-west Europe in general, they tended to leave school slightly earlier. Since 1957–8 the United Kingdom average leaving age has undoubtedly increased due to the voluntary enrolment trends noted earlier, but concomitant trends have been evident in other European countries also, so the relative position of the United Kingdom has hardly improved. This is borne out by a quality index of the education of the labour force constructed by Denison, adjusting for number of hours and days spent in school, absenteeism, etc., and taking 1950 as a base. The result is as follows:

Quality index of growth of education of labour force 1950–62

(1950=100)	1950	1955	1960	1962
U.S.A.	100	103·3	107·4	109·0
Northwestern Europe	100	101·8	103·6	104·5
United Kingdom	100	102·1	104·4	105·5

The United Kingdom slightly improved its position relative to the rest of Europe, but lagged behind the U.S.A. to a much greater extent. A more detailed comparison shows that the United Kingdom was behind Belgium, France and Italy, but ahead of Denmark, Germany, the Netherlands and Norway. Italy is not included in the above table; its inclusion would narrow the improvement which has occurred in Britain's position relative to that of the rest of Europe.

Overall, then, a measure such as raising the school leaving age, especially when its probable secondary effects of increasing enrolments at higher ages are taken into account, should lead to an increase in the number of years of education given on average to members of the labour force. This general education may not be of direct vocational importance, but it almost certainly does improve the adaptability and perhaps the mobility of the labour force – factors which are important in a growing economy.

But it is hardly possible to argue from the evidence given here that there is some economic imperative for raising the school leaving age. Still less are there grounds for the often-made assertion of the type: 'Our economic growth rate depends on a higher rate of investment, especially investment in education. If we are not to lag even more behind the rest of Europe and the U.S.A. in economic growth, we must increase our educational effort generally, and especially increase the school leaving age.' Such assertions have no basis in fact. It is arguable that our educational system has not in many respects lagged behind the rest of Western Europe. Some general association may well exist between levels of economic and educational development; it does not follow that the expansion of a particular kind of education will make the economy grow faster. These negative statements should illustrate the essentially subordinate role that the economist has to play in deciding educational policy. The real reasons for raising the school leaving age are surely social and cultural, if anything. One important cost (which it was estimated was far greater than the direct, visible public expenditure involved) was the effect of withdrawing a large number from the labour force. This leads one to ask whether or not the money involved would be better spent on vocational training, whether on or off the job, and whether full- or part-time? The answer to this also goes far beyond the realm of economics, but the question is surely worthwhile asking if one considers the low motivation of children aged 15 whose presence in school is not voluntary.

REFERENCES

1 *Education and Science in 1968*, Cmnd. 3950, H.M.S.O., p. 11.

2 Independent, direct grant and special schools will account for nearly 10% of the age-group, leaving about 90% in maintained schools. This is analogous to the present enrolment pattern of 14-year-olds. It is a reasonable assumption that maintained schools only will be affected by the change. The effect on independent and special schools should be negligible.

3 It is interesting to note that before the extent of increasing voluntary enrolment in recent years became apparent, the estimated increase in enrolments due to the raising of the school leaving age in 1970–1 had been estimated at 500,000. See J. Vaizey, *The Control of Education*, London, 1960, p. 136.

4 'Opportunity cost' means the cost of a certain course of action (in this case compulsory enrolment) over an alternative course. As the latter (voluntary enrolment) will be hypothetical, so too will the opportunity cost be hypothetical.

5 The projections are taken from Department of Education and Science reports and from *Statistics of Education*.

6 The details of the current-cost projections were as follows: average current cost per pupil in secondary schools was £143 in 1966. Deducting loan charges of £19·1 per pupil, average *direct* current cost per pupil was £123·9. This figure was the basis for projections, as direct expenditures (on teachers, books, ancillary staff, lighting, heating, etc.) are likely to vary directly with the number of pupils. Costs for pupils aged less than 16 were probably lower than the overall average (due to high costs of sixth-formers), and taking into account (*a*) off-set costs paid by L.E.A.s for education of pupils outside their area and (*b*) the proportion of sixth-formers, it seemed necessary to reduce the overall direct unit costs by 10% to get a figure applicable to the under-16s, i.e. £111·5 in 1966.

The next step was to allow for the effects of changes in the pupil-teacher ratio. This ratio was 18·4:1 in all maintained secondary schools in 1966, according to *Statistics of Education*, 1966, Vol. I. The inclusion of sixth forms imparts a bias to this ratio, but the bias is not large; for instance, the pupil-teacher ratio in secondary modern schools was 19·4:1 in 1966. Furthermore, changes in teacher supply will probably affect all types of schools and classes equally, and therefore the global ratio of 18·4:1 is a reasonable basis for projection, especially when the trend towards more comprehensive education is taken into account. On this basis 16·1:1 is taken as the pupil-teacher ratio for 1972–3. This is derived from enrolment estimates given in *Statistics of Education*, 1966, Vol. I, table 44, and an interpolation of teacher forecasts given for 1972 and 1976 in the Ninth Report of the National Advisory Council on the training and supply of teachers (*The Demand for and Supply of Teachers 1963–1986*, H.M.S.O., 1965). This reduction of the pupil-teacher ratio will, of itself, increase teaching cost per pupil by 10·8%.

Finally, the increase in *per capita* national income between 1966 and 1973, which is a major cost-increasing item, must be allowed for. It will be assumed here that (*a*) teachers' incomes will change at the same rate as income per head generally (i.e. that teachers will maintain their position in the income hierarchy), (*b*) that the non-teacher items in current costs will also increase at the same rate as income per head, and (*c*) that national income will increase at 2% per annum between 1966 and 1973. (Setting a figure for this increase

Economic aspects 69

is hazardous, as previous Government and private attempts have shown. However, low as 2% may seem, it should be remembered that it is fairly close to the actual 1966–7 rate of growth, and that previous estimates have tended to be over-optimistic. It should be remembered that we are talking in real terms, i.e. 1966 prices, throughout.)

These assumptions mean that teaching cost per pupil will rise between 1966 and 1973 by 27·3%, i.e. compounding the effects of higher incomes and lower pupil-teacher ratios. Non-teaching costs should rise by 14·9%. Thus the aggregate increase in direct current costs should be 23·3% (i.e. the weighted average of the component rates). This implies average direct costs per pupil of £137·5, and average current (including indirect) costs of £165. Multiplying by the number of extra pupils (287,000), total current costs are £48·5m. and total direct costs £39·5m.

7 See *Public Expenditure in 1968–69 and 1969–70*, Cmnd. 3515, H.M.S.O., 1968. The Government expenditure forecasts exclude capital expenditure of nationalized industries.

8 For an extensive analysis of the relationship between 'on-the-job' training and earnings see Becker, G. S., *Human Capital*, New York: Natioanal Bureau of Economic Research, 1964.

9 See, for instance, Floud, Jean, and Halsey, A. H., 'English Secondary Schools and the Supply of Labour' in *The Yearbook of Education, 1956*, London, 1956.

10 There are slightly more boys than girls because the larger participation in voluntary enrolment by boys (less than 1% greater than for girls) it is outweighed by the larger number of boys in the 1973 population projection for 15-year-olds.

11 See Denison, E. F., assisted by Poullier, Jean-Pierre, *Why Growth Rates Differ*, The Brokings Institution, Washington, D.C., 1967; also Aukrust, Odd, 'Investment and Economic Growth', *Productivity Measurement Review*, February 1959.

12 Jorgenson, D. W., and Griliches, Z., 'The Explanation of Productivity Change', *Review of Economic Studies*, xxxiv (3), No. 99, July 1967.

13 See Becker, G. S., op. cit. chs. 3–6; Renshaw, E. F., 'Estimating the Returns to Education', *Review of Economics and Statistics*, xlii, August 1960; Schultz, T. W., 'Investment in Human Capital', *American Economic Review*, li, March 1961.

14 'An Economic Interpretation of the Private Demand for Education', *Economica*, N.S., 33, May 1966.

5 The further education option

Tyrrell Burgess

Whatever the arguments for raising the school leaving age, one question that is increasingly asked is: must the last year of compulsory education be spent in school? At present most young people over 15 who are getting any education at all are getting it, not in schools, but in further education – in technical colleges, colleges of technology, commerce and so on. What the table shows is that

Pupils aged 15 and over in education of all kinds, January 1967, thousands

	15 under S.L.A. (School leaving age)	15 over S.L.A.	Total 15	16	17	18	19	Total 15–19 (excl. those under S.L.A.)
Maintained schools	188	190	379	162	87	31	3	473
% of the age-group	28·7	29·1	57·8	23·9	12·2	4·1	0·4	9·5
All schools	206	224	430	202	114	40	4	585
% of the age-group	31·4	34·2	65·6	29·9	16·0	5·3	0·5	12·1 (cont.)

(cont.)	15 under S.L.A.	15 over S.L.A.	Total 15	16	17	18	19	Total 15–19 (excl. those under S.L.A.)
Full-time further education (incl. sandwich)			15	39	37	30	25	
Part-time further education			45	104	126	105	84	
Further education, evening only			22	39	49	47	43	
Total further education excl. evening institutes			82	182	212	182	151	809
% of the age-group			12·5	26·9	29·9	24·0	17·9	27·1
Nos. at evening institutes			134	67	59	45	39	

Source: D.E.S. Statistics of Ed., 1967, Vol. 3
Note: I am indebted for this table to Miss Patricia Hughes.

young people vote with their feet. Because of the existence of two school leaving dates in the year, the table actually conceals the fact that about half of all young people leave school at the earliest legal age. By the time the picture becomes clearer, with the 16-year-olds, the colleges can be seen to be accommodating nearly as many pupils as the schools, and thereafter they rapidly surpass the schools. The colleges even make a significant contribution to the kind of education which the schools pre-eminently offer. One in five of all candidates for the G.C.E. at A and O levels enters from the colleges. It is not surprising that many people in education have looked at these figures and wondered whether a school leaving age of 16 should necessarily imply that young people should spend the extra time in schools.

The reasons why young people may wish to leave school are many and various. It may be just the general restlessness of adolescence, the need for novelty and change. This may be exacerbated by personal difficulties, such as a dislike of a particular teacher or frustration at not being able to get a course one wants. These personal difficulties are bound to arise and it is a good thing that there are alternative ways of getting an education.

Although opportunities in secondary education are growing all the time, there are still some small schools, even grammar schools, which cannot offer a very wide range of subjects. There are still some secondary modern schools which cannot offer subjects at the required level. And even when comprehensive reorganization is nearing completion, there must still be subjects which most schools do not tackle and for which most young people still go to the technical colleges. But the schools may also restrict opportunity, almost unwittingly. All over secondary education pupils find themselves faced with choices in the curriculum. They may have to choose between two modern languages or whether or not to drop geography, or a particular bias in science. At any stage a pupil may find his possibilities in school limited by the fact that he has dropped some crucial subject earlier on. At the same time the schools tend to advise pupils not to attempt courses, particularly those leading to examinations, where they do not see any chance of success. Both of these kinds of 'drop out' may find themselves in a technical college. Colleges have traditionally seen themselves as offering a second chance. Many of them take students who have been told by their schools that they cannot manage two A levels in two years and get them through three A levels in one.

They are helped in this by the fact that the student may feel he has some incentive to succeed in order to prove an earlier judgment of schools or parents wrong. Many students respond well to finding themselves no longer in compulsory education: they themselves are choosing to be in the colleges and to take the courses.

And, of course, the atmosphere of the colleges can be quite different from that of the schools. Most obviously, the colleges are not filled with younger children. Indeed the 15- or 16-year-old will be one of the younger college students and will see older – sometimes very much older – people in the same institution continuing their education. The atmosphere of the colleges is simply more adult. The 16-year-old becomes a student, not a pupil. He comes and goes as he pleases and is not faced with regulations about dress, deportment and so on, which seem increasingly nonsensical.

But perhaps most young people who leave school early do so, not for personal or academic reasons, but for economic ones. What seems most important to them is to get out and earn a living, both for their own purposes and to help their family budget. It is for these young people that the technical colleges are of the greatest importance, because they offer a chance to continue education in the evenings or on a part-time basis. The importance of this can be seen from the figures in the table. It still is the case that the maintenance of educational opportunity for working-class youngsters depends wholly upon the technical colleges. The arduous and unsatisfactory part-time route to the highest qualifications is essential to the preservation of opportunity.

It is not too much to say that what young people are revealing when they go to technical colleges is the existence of two recognizably distinct traditions of education in Great Britain. The first, which is very familiar to educated people, is the academic tradition represented by the grammar school and the university. This is an exclusive tradition, reflected not only in educational practice, but in administrative arrangements. It is concerned at heart with knowledge 'for its own sake'. The universities say that they are concerned with the preservation, extension and dissemination of knowledge. They concentrate as much upon research as upon teaching. Hence the importance of the individual subject and subject department. Hence too the fact that university people do not seek to justify their studies in external terms. The studies are their own justification. They are not, and indeed should not be, defined in terms of their usefulness or relevance or social necessity. Given this, it is very clear that universities have to be very careful about the people they admit, so they have rigid and incidentally ever stiffer entry requirements. So it has been necessary for the universities to make demands upon the grammar schools which have effectively determined the latter's curriculum at least from the age of 14 and probably earlier. It is only now, with comprehensive reorganization, that we are giving up the early part of the admission process to universities, which was the elimination of three-quarters of the population at the age of 11 plus from any effective access to a university education. The British universities have placed high value upon early academic attainment and thus upon early specialization. They are driven to this, not by class hatred or conscious ill-will, but by their view of what constitutes learning.

It is this too, which leads to rigidity in the kinds of course offered. The overwhelming majority of courses in British universities are from three to four years long, are pursued in full-time study and lead to an honours first degree. The process here has been inexorable, driven by pressure from numbers of applicants on the one hand and the explosion of human knowledge on the other. Entry standards have risen steadily. The pass or general degree has been devalued or abandoned. A second degree, even more specialized than the first, is becoming more common.

The consequence of the universities' exclusiveness, their concentration on full-time study, their insistence upon particular entry qualifications have ensured that they remain the preserve largely of the middle classes. It is still something of a shock to realize that the proportion of university students with working-class parents is the same today (about one quarter) as it was in 1928.

There are two other consequences of the academic tradition. The first is that the institutions devoted to it are educationally conservative. The greatest changes in education in the last half-century have come in those areas which are remotest from the opinion of the universities (the primary schools) or in those institutions (such as the technical colleges) which are controlled by local authorities. The academic tradition does not respond quickly to the changing needs of society. The grammar schools can change slightly: after 1944 they accepted not only the relatively rich, but the relatively clever. But they were not able to contribute to the task of offering secondary education for all, including the relatively poor and the relatively stupid – and so attempts to provide secondary education for all involve either the destruction of the grammar schools or such change as to render them unrecognizable.

Similarly, universities cannot move quickly to meet obvious social needs such as the training of large numbers of technologists or of mathematics and science teachers for schools. They cannot, at the same time, do what they believe in and meet the increasing demand for places for potential students. If we are to offer higher education for all before the end of this century, the universities will have either to be abolished or to be changed out of all recognition. The second implication of the academic tradition is institutional independence. The University Grants Committee is the most obvious arrangement for achieving this, but the existence of aided status in schools is in effect another. The existence of the latter makes secondary education for all difficult to achieve, even with the best will in the world (which is sometimes lacking).

This academic tradition in education may be the most familiar to middle-class parents, to journalists and commentators, and indeed to most people in education. But it is not the only one. The alternative tradition, which is quite as venerable, is exemplified by the technical colleges. An attempt was made, half-hearted and ultimately abortive though it was, to make it the basis of the secondary modern schools after 1944. The essence of this tradition is not the pursuit of knowledge for its own sake, but the pursuit of 'useful' knowledge – in other words, professional and vocational education. The colleges are used to justifying what they do, not so much in its own terms as in its relevance to society, to industry and to the needs of students. They are used to responding to social and industrial demand. If a local firm approaches a college with a request for a course of training – at almost any level – the college will seek to provide it. If many thousands of young people, baulked of a university place, turn to the colleges, the colleges respond, expanding as they do so far beyond technical subjects into the arts and social sciences.

All this means that the technical colleges are not exclusive in the same way as universities and grammar schools are. Their habit is to take all-comers. They are, in effect, 'comprehensive' institutions. Naturally, individual courses of study may have some stated entry requirement, but the college as a whole does not. A technical college may in fact have an almost bewildering variety of level of courses and mode of study. It is not just that the colleges offer both O levels and degrees – even higher degrees. They also offer courses whose academic content is relatively low and which are stigmatized as 'mere' vocational training for semi-skilled occupations. The range of subjects is quite as wide – from hairdressing or shorthand for 15-year-olds to engineering or economics. And they take students of all ages, from 15-year-old school-leavers to 25-year-olds doing degree courses and much older people on all kinds of training and re-training. Their students come to them for full-time and sandwich courses, part-time, released from their jobs perhaps one day a week, or in the evening only. In other words, the student body in a technical college is quite different from the homogeneous group in universities, in age, length of course, subject and mode of study, and so on.

The consequence of all this is that the technical colleges represent the normal route for post-school educational qualifications for working-class people. In offering chances at all levels to those who have dropped out of the academic route at 11, 15, 16 or some other age, and in offering them in ways which can be combined with earning a living, the technical colleges keep open perhaps the only route of its kind.

Part of the attraction is that this route is vocationally relevant. In a university even those subjects which might be thought to be vocationally biased, such as engineering, law, medicine, are not taught in such a way that the student is a qualified person at the end of the course. He requires a further period of practical experience. It was the technical colleges which pioneered the 'sandwich' course, in which periods of industrial practice were an integral part of the academic course. And the colleges are still pioneering here by extending this principle, not only in science and engineering, but in the social sciences.

As if to underline their social responsiveness, the technical colleges have normally been public institutions, maintained by the local authorities. They are administered, in other words, under the same arrangements as primary and secondary schools. They are not 'autonomous' institutions like universities. This is held to inhibit their independence, and so it does in many respects. On the other hand, it is worth remembering that under the National Certificate schemes created in the 1920s technical colleges were creating courses and setting and marking examinations with a national validity, at a time when new university colleges could not create their own degree courses, but were limited to the degrees of the University of London.

These, then, are our two traditions of education – and, of course, there are many people who will say that I have made the distinction too clear-cut and over-simplified. There are some university courses which are vocational and some technical college courses which are academic in both the best and worst senses. But nobody looking at the history of British education during the last hundred years or more can doubt that the two traditions exist, that each has its value and attractiveness and that they are recognizably devoted to different ideals and different goals.

The question is which of them is most appropriate to those young people legally compelled to stay on at school until they are 16 when, without compulsion, they would probably have left? There is no need to think of this question in extreme terms. We only need to ask what should be the tendency of the educational experience which is offered. There is little doubt about the answer of the young people themselves. Recently the Schools Council commissioned an Inquiry from the Government Social Survey on the interests and motives of pupils between the ages of 13 and 16 and their views on what the schools were doing to prepare them for adult life. It also sought to show how much teachers knew about what was relevant to pupils, and parents' views about their own and the schools' roles in education.

One of the first questions the Survey set out to answer was what pupils, parents and teachers thought a school was for. A sample of 15-year-old school-leavers and their parents were asked which of a number of objectives of schools they considered very important. Very broadly speaking, most 15-year-olds thought objectives concerned with careers to be very important. Slightly fewer of them thought that other practical aspects of everyday life, such as money management and running a home, were very important. Slightly fewer again rated highly the objective of self-development (becoming independent, making the most of oneself and so on). Only about one in three of the children rated highly the objective of broadening the mind and developing interests and awareness.

The opinions of parents on the whole were very similar to those of the pupils – except that 91% of parents put 'teach you to be able to put things in writing easily' as very important. On the whole more parents thought that all school objectives were important than did their children.

The views of teachers on the other hand were a direct contrast. Most of them claimed aspects of self-development as very important and many of them chose from the interest and awareness group. Only half or fewer thought that school objectives related to careers were important. The contrast represents that between the academic tradition of learning for its own sake, favoured by the teachers, and the vocational tradition, favoured by the pupils. From the Inquiry it seems that teachers recognize this and are uneasy about it, because the great majority of teachers said they thought that school subjects should where possible be linked to pupils' lives outside school, so that pupils could see the value of the subjects. On the other hand, when asked what new elements teachers hoped to introduce into their teaching when the school leaving age was raised, the largest group of answers concerned things intended to widen the pupils' interests, to develop their aesthetic appreciation, to make them self-sufficient and generally to enrich their lives. In other words, the teachers hoped to use the longer secondary school course to offer the pupils more of what the pupils considered unimportant.

It is this difference of educational attitude, rather than the more transient problems of personal difficulty or lack of provision, which provides the chief respectable justification for turning to the technical colleges as part of the attempt to offer a full secondary education for all.

It is something of a let-down, after all this, to discover that very few local authorities are actually planning to use the technical colleges to help to increase opportunities in secondary education – even for pupils beyond the school leaving age. The chief reason for this is the unhelpful state of the law. The Education Act 1944 says (Section 36) that it is the duty of parents to see that children of compulsory school age get efficient full-time education suitable to their age, ability and aptitudes, 'either by regular attendance at school or otherwise'. If one looks at this section in isolation one might conclude that 'or otherwise' could include a technical college. But things are not so simple. The Education Act also provides (in Section 7) that there shall be three progressive stages of education: primary, secondary and further. Further education (which is what goes on in technical colleges) is defined as education 'for persons over compulsory school age' (Section 41): which means that by definition a person of compulsory school age cannot be educated in a technical college.

This legal fact is reflected in administrative practice. A local education authority is likely to have sub-committees for primary, secondary and further education: it might even divide the duties of deputy or assistant education officers along these lines. It can thus be only after a conscious effort to think beyond the administrative framework that a local authority can plan, as it were, across the boundaries of responsibility.

Of course, neither laws nor administrative practices are unchangeable. In response to a recommendation of the Plowden Committee on primary schools, and under the practical pressure to make the best use of existing school buildings for secondary reorganization, a number of authorities sought to establish 'middle' schools, taking children from the age of 8 or 9 to 13 or 14 and thus straddling the division between primary and secondary education. The Education Act 1964 made it possible for them to do this, and there are now middle schools established in perhaps six local authorities. Comparable legislation could certainly be introduced to abolish the boundaries between the secondary and further stages of education, though here there would have to be a great deal more amendment of regulations as well. But the law could be changed, and the expectation is that in any new Education Act it would be.

On the other hand, it is not enough to have a good idea and follow it through to legislation. Life is rarely entirely simple, and the thoughtless solution of one problem can awkwardly create others. The doubts arise from the very phrase, 'further education option', which is what the proposal is called to make education for the last compulsory years available in technical colleges. Baldly the questions are: Who is the option for? What options are being offered?

We have met options before in education. There are still some people who assert, and may even believe, that there is an element of choice in the arrangements for selection which are made at 11 plus. – as if anyone could choose a grammar school, or as if many people actually did choose a secondary modern. We have also seen how, as the 11 plus became increasingly unpopular, local authorities began to minimize their public emphasis on tests and to assert that parents would be able to choose the secondary school to which their child was to go. The choice, of course, was to be 'guided' by heads and other teachers. One does not need to be totally cynical to detect in all this simply another method of selection.

So the first question that arises is whether the further education option means what many of its supporters want it to mean, a genuine opportunity for young people and their parents to choose a course appropriate to them. If we are to institutionalize a form of selection at 14 or 15 plus we should at least know what we are doing – not suddenly find that we have done so by mistake. Neither must we forget that a subtle process of rejection is taking place in the schools all the time. As the Schools Council Inquiry found, there is a very wide divergence between those who leave school as soon as possible and the teachers who have been teaching them on what a school is basically about. It is natural that teachers should find it harder to interest those who reject their values and persuade them on the value of additional education. The very act of raising the school leaving age has been a great stimulus in making many teachers think again about the purposes of education. Indeed, the process of raising the age has been an almost classic example of announcing a reform before people were 'ready' for it and by the very announcement startling them into readiness. The Schools

Council Inquiry is simply one example of a large number of ways in which teachers, faced with the possibility of large numbers of children staying at school longer because the law says so, have sought to understand the needs and wishes of these older pupils. This effort has been especially necessary among those teachers in comprehensive schools whose experience has hitherto been mostly concerned with those academic children who have stayed on voluntarily. The attitudes and practices of secondary schools cannot but benefit from this kind of fundamental thinking, however induced. The obvious fear about the further-education option is that it will enable teachers in schools to pass on to their colleagues in technical colleges precisely those pupils who cause them most thought. Again, we shall come to see if we are not careful a set of arrangements whose basis, though ostensibly educational, is effectively social. It does not require too world-weary a view of British social habits to predict that the children who will be found suitable for education in the tech. are the children of manual workers.

A second doubt arises from contrasts in provision. For a choice to be real it has to be between comparable alternatives. A choice between better and worse is no choice at all. Already the contrast in the physical provision for those who stay on at school and those who leave is stark. The former are in an institution specifically designed for them, pursuing courses of work of their own choice. As part of their normal day, they have access to libraries, playing fields, gymnasia and so on. Outside the normal time-table there may be clubs and societies to suit all interests. Not all schools are equally good or equally well provided for, but the 17-year-old at school is thought without too much question to need a pretty lavish physical provision. For his contemporary at work no such effort is thought necessary. He quite simply lacks what the older schoolboy takes for granted. Even if he is getting some sort of part-time education in a technical college, he will not find around him, as a matter of course, the same provision as would be available at school. So whatever the arguments might be for the more adult atmosphere of the colleges and the difference in their educational traditions, we must be quite sure that the further-education option does not mean simply offering young people less.

The signs are not encouraging. The technical college tradition of taking all-comers, including drop-outs, from the rest of the educational service, is an honourable and even glorious one, but politicians, administrators and people in the rest of education seem to have got the view that the techs. will manage regardless. It is no coincidence that during the next few years, when the colleges will be urged to accommodate vastly growing numbers of 18-year-olds who cannot get into university, together with a whole lot of 15- and 16-year-olds turfed out of the schools, the resources available to technical colleges are being much more severely limited than those for any other sector of education. The further-education option can so easily become just the latest device for keeping the workers' children in their place.

Can we avoid the disadvantages? Is the further-education option bound to be a cheat? Must British education always talk in terms of dividing and selecting? The analogy of the middle schools may be helpful here. With them, the blurring of the distinction between the primary and secondary stages has been achieved by the creation of institutions, to which all children go as a matter of course and which differ in their age-range, but not in the educational or social background of their pupils. Things are more complicated with older pupils. The range of courses available, the variety of subject choice, the differences of interest provoked by likely jobs, all demand a much more complex institution. But the principle remains. What we need is a comprehensive college for the under-18s. Pupils would go to such a college at 14 or 15 and would have available to them the whole range of opportunities open to them now in schools, plus those which many of them would take up after the school leaving age. The college would offer not only O level and C.S.E., but a whole range of technical and vocational courses. After a school leaving age of 16, many of the children would, of course, stay on full-time to take an A level and to apply for university entrance. Others would stay on full-time to do either academic or vocational courses. And it would still be open to those children who had left at the school leaving age to come back into the college part-time and in the evenings. In other words, they would be kept in touch with the education service, through their college, until they were 18. The college and its facilities would be available to them whether they were taking full-time or part-time courses – and even if they were taking no courses at all. Such an institution would not be the academic 'sixth-form college' which some educators had advocated; nor would it have simply the vocational and indeed remedial function of the technical colleges; nor would it much resemble the old, dead idea of a county college, to which young people would be released part-time for cultural improvement. It would be a combination of all of these things, and in the combination much more.

I myself would hope that all the courses, full-time and part-time, would have a common core of subjects without which living in the modern world is increasingly difficult: these would include maths, English, science, psychology, sociology and economics. And one wonders if it could be anything but beneficial for full-timers and part-timers to find themselves in the same classes for these common-core subjects.

This is only a sketch of what the educational basis of such a comprehensive college might be. Of course, each institution would work its ideals and practices through for itself. All the administrators can do (as with secondary reorganization) is to create the conditions in which teachers can offer the greatest opportunities to the greatest numbers and in which pupils and parents have the greatest range of flexibility and choice. With the existence of such colleges as I have described, one could be reasonably confident that the further-education option would be a reality. Without it, or something like it, we could look forward without surprise to the education system's creation of yet further opportunities for teachers to encourage the fortunate and succour the well-to-do.

6   A headmaster's point of view

Albert Rowe

One cannot adequately come to grips with the effect on the schools of the extra year and what ought to be done unless one considers at the outset why the postponement of the raising of the school leaving age was publicly welcomed by many teachers and privately greeted with such heartfelt sighs of relief by so very many more.

The first reason is also the most obvious. It's the same now as it was when the Minister of Education accepted the recommendation of the *Newsom Report* that the school leaving age should be raised to 16 for all pupils entering the secondary school from September 1965, later postponed to 1970, later – and by a Labour Government! – postponed to 1972. It is that the extra buildings, facilities, and equipment will not in fact be available in 1972 to cope with the increase in numbers.

The second reason is that the extra teachers will not be available: not only the extra ones to handle the increase in numbers on the present national secondary-school ratio of one teacher to about 19 pupils, but also to give a better teacher-pupil ratio than this – a ratio of, say, at least one to 15. For whatever else is in dispute, it is clear to those who will have to do the job that when the whole ability range of pupils is in school for the full fifth year some of the groups will have to be smaller than the existing ones, consisting, as these mostly do, of pupils voluntarily staying on for examination courses.

First, smaller because the heartening yearly increase in the total number taking worthwhile examinations will be speeded up, helped by the continuing steady improvement in the examinations themselves, and a proportion of these pupils will need more individual attention if they are to succeed: something pupils of similar ability have always had in the private sector because their parents could afford to pay for it, and which explains the remarkable success of some private schools in preparing for O and A level and university entrance pupils who at 11 plus were judged incapable of profiting from an examination course. You may deprecate the inexorable trend towards more pupils taking more examinations. This was the stance of the 1963 *Newsom Report*, which would 'strongly champion the right of any school to abstain altogether from public examinations if the head and staff were convinced that the best interests of the pupils required this'. Nowhere in education – a subject sodden with it – is it more necessary to clear one's mind of cant than here. By altering the nature, content, and techniques of examinations (see p. 91), not abolishing them for 'the others', as those with plenty of examination qualifications are so fond of advocating, our aim should be to ensure that more and more pupils can be successful. Parallel with this, and even more important, our total assessment of a pupil should be made so many-sided, so all-embracing, as to ensure that examination results play only their proper part and no more, thus preventing them from continuing to be what they have become – the stigmata of a meritocratic *elite*.

Second, smaller groups also – and this is of crucial importance – because the fifth-year non-examination pupils, diminishing though their number will be as we learn how to motivate them and teach them better, will present problems which if not solved could disrupt the work of the fifth year and indeed of the whole school and which, leaving out the few exceptional schools, can only be solved if they are able to be taught in groups of a dozen to fifteen. To the truth so memorably put by the 1959 *Crowther Report*, 'There is no escape from the fact that below-average children make above-average demands on the educational system', one must from experience add: *demands that increase in complexity and grow more taxing the older they are.*

The potential threat presented by this particular problem has caused many educationists as well as teachers, whose goodwill is not in question, to doubt the wisdom of raising the school leaving age. Why introduce compulsion when voluntary staying on is increasing so satisfactorily? And are not education and compulsion contradictory?

While sympathizing with their point of view, I utterly reject it. Both the *Crowther Report* and the 1963 *Robbins Report* emphasized that our society would not be able to achieve its desired economic growth and higher cultural standards unless, to quote Robbins, it used its 'large reservoirs of untapped ability in the population'. Both reports make clear that this untapped ability exists chiefly among children of the working classes. And these, as dedicated teachers know from bitter experience and as is now conclusively proved by the *National Survey of Health and Development* carried out by Dr J. W. B. Douglas and his colleagues, are the very pupils who leave school as soon as possible. They must therefore be kept in school if society is to achieve its twin objectives of economic growth and higher cultural standards as put forward by Crowther and Robbins.

Culture, like morality, is a relative thing: there are as many cultures as there are people. The phrase 'higher cultural standards' is consequently, as it stands, meaningless. I prefer to express society's twin objectives somewhat differently. First, economic growth: yes, provided that we keep asking ourselves, 'Growth for what?' Second, the development of greater awareness of, and sensitivity towards, each other and springing from this, a truer sense of community. This would help to ensure, among other things, that Government was urgently charged with the task of using part of the fruits of economic growth to provide more and more substantial and equitable opportunities for every citizen, if he wishes, to lead the good life and to raise the quality of his own living.

Pupils, then, should be kept in compulsorily for the extra year; and as many as possible voluntarily thereafter if they are to contribute to society's economic growth all they are capable of. Kept in for their own sakes also: surely the true prize of education is life itself, and a longer education will help them to raise the quality of their living both in school and out, now and later, and to lead a happier, more useful, more satisfactory and fulfilled life.

Extra teachers are certainly required. Ideally, teachers who have been trained to meet the special demands that the pupils we've been discussing will make on them – those hitherto considered as non-academic and who'll increasingly be taking examinations, and those who, however few they become as time goes on, will at least for the foreseeable future be non-academic and who will need time and effort and concern out of all proportion to their numbers. The fact that such specially-trained, mature teachers will not be available, or if available not in the required quantity, is another reason many head teachers and their staffs do not welcome the extra year.

The simple but nevertheless unpalatable truth is that the extra year, with certain modifications and extensions for the pupils we have been concentrating on, can only be an extension of the education all pupils have had in previous years. If each pupil has in his own way been reasonably happy in the first four secondary years, and reasonably hard-working and successful, judged solely by what he at his best is capable of, then this can be extended into his fifth year. Put bluntly, those who most fuss about and fear the extra year are tacitly admitting that the kind of education they have been able to provide hasn't been of this kind. In such cases the problem of what to do with the extra year can only be solved by first altering the education given earlier. It is the lack of recognition of this that vitiates so much discussion and writing on the subject. The point needs stressing: the extra year (and the further education I hope will follow it) will only make sense if it is firmly based on what has gone before.

What kind of education must be given earlier if the extra year is to be a natural, welcome, and successful extension of it? We can most satisfactorily arrive at an answer by first noting what the two most important post-war pieces of educational research tell us. Both are longitudinal studies, both concerned with home and school.

That of Dr Douglas and his colleagues, already referred to, was based on a representative sample of 5,000 children studied from birth to 21 years of age. In their latest book, *All Our Future*[1], which covers the first five secondary-school years, they show how the expressed intention of the 1944 Act to give each child, irrespective of his family circumstances and social origins, a secondary education 'suitable to his age, ability, and aptitude' has been frustrated.

'Middle-class pupils have retained, almost intact', they say,

> their historic advantage over the manual working class. . . . Thus nearly half the lower manual working-class pupils of high ability have left school before they are sixteen and a half years. Early leaving and low job aspirations make it probable that as many as 5 per cent of the next generation of manual workers will be recruited from pupils who, in other circumstances, might have qualified for administrative or professional occupations. . . . Both parental interest and school staffing and equipment are associated with age of leaving. These two factors are, of course, highly correlated, but neither adequately compensates for the deficiency of the other – the interest of the parents alone is insufficient to counter the deficiencies of the schools.

The other and complementary longitudinal study was made by Professor Himmelweit and her colleagues.[2] It was of 600 middle- and working-class adolescents, 13 to 14 years old, who were studied again when they were 25. The adolescents were from four grammar and five secondary modern schools, so the study was of the effects, good and bad, intended and unintended, of the bipartite system. The results of the study were clear, Himmelweit says, and are backed up by those of international research. 'Information about the type of school a child attends enables better prediction of his behaviour, outlook, values and attainments than does information about his I.Q. or his family's background.' And even within the grammar school the stream to which a pupil is assigned – A, B, C or D – affects his ultimate performance, and therefore his life-chance, more than does his ability or motivation.

> Analysis of the adult data confirmed the findings obtained in adolescence – namely, that school rather than home affected the individual's subsequent occupational history, job-level and aspirations. Moreover, his evaluation of his own career achievements was determined far more by reference to the achievements of his classmates than to those of his family.

Middle-class parents know this. Consequently, they rightly see the direction of their children to a secondary modern school as a threat to their life-chance. This goes a good way towards explaining both the support of those with 11-plus borderline or below-borderline children for the comprehensive school and of those with above-borderline children for the grammar school. They also recognize the crucial nature of the decision to put their children into any other stream than A, even in a grammar or a comprehensive school. But because streaming is still unfortunately so widespread as to merit being called an education system in miniature',[3] they see no way out.

To sum up: The problem of the extra year must be seen as part of the problem of secondary education as a whole. To keep those pupils who would have left at 15 in school for another year will only be effective if their previous experience of education has been of the right kind. The extra year should also make a quite fundamental contribution towards rendering untrue Crowther's statement, shaming to such a rich country as ours: 'The report is about the education of boys and girls aged from 15 to 18. Most of them are not being educated.' This it will only do if, by the quality of the education it offers, it retains voluntarily in school beyond the extra year a large proportion of that half of the working-class pupils of high ability

Douglas points out at present leave before they are 16½. These are the pupils who chiefly provide, in the phrase already quoted from Robbins, the 'large reservoirs of untapped ability in the population'. Douglas and his colleagues, by proving that the social advantages middle-class have over working-class pupils are as great as ever, bring home to us the fact that the problem of how to make the most of the latter's talents has not yet been solved, while underlining as a prerequisite the necessity of the 'best staffing and the best equipment'. (And it must be interpolated here that to remove these social disadvantages even in part would need, as well as changing the schools, a massive compensatory programme of housing, health and welfare, and adult education in which the powerful mass media at present so little used for anything of value would be used to the full). Himmelweit and her colleagues demonstrate how important for the life-chance of the pupil is the type of school and stream in what is still largely a bipartite system.

The basic question to be answered, then, is this: What is the right kind of education in the first four years which will result, not only in a worthwhile further year for those who at present leave at 15, but also in keeping voluntarily in school thereafter the greater proportion of high-ability working-class pupils who leave at 16½?

The basic answer follows from Professor Himmelweit's statement at the 1969 Cambridge Teach-in: 'I would say we have a system which is probably unique in the world in the sense that we groom for failure as assiduously as we groom for success.' It's this. Only when schools stop grooming for failure, stop rejecting the majority for the supposed sake of an academic minority, and transform themselves from rejecting into accepting schools in which, in the words of Michael Young, pupils can 'develop at their own pace to their own particular fulfilment' will our problem be on the way to being solved.[4] Make no mistake about it. Working-class pupils, and not only them, are sickened by school and driven out of it by a one-dimensional competitive concept of achievement and success that is an exact reflection of acquisitive middle-class values, of the 'rat race', held even more firmly by teachers of working-class than of middle-class origin – the familiar rejection syndrome. As a consequence, these pupils find themselves culturally alienated, up against a barrier which the majority cannot cross and which the minority are able to cross only by damaging themselves, cutting themselves off from their roots, and becoming even more competitive, acquisitive and philistine than their models.[5]

The majority of working-class pupils, then, fail to respond to middle-class socialization simply because they cannot. Behaviour is a function of experience; as we experience the world, so will we behave. A working-class pupil's life-style is the result of his experience. If it is rejected, then inevitably will he feel himself to be, and will in turn reject the rejectors. To keep him in school, one has to accept that working-class culture, values, life-style are as valid as middle-class. But this would mean changing teachers' attitudes about their pupils. And those attitudes are, as I've shown, so deeply class and socially conditioned as to be unconscious and therefore very difficult to change – in pupils as well as teachers.[6] So pupils live up to, or down to, the labels of their school streams – A, B, C, D. And how can teachers be made so aware of their own assumptions, their own culture-relativity, that they are able to detach themselves sufficiently to accept a pupil on his own terms? In fellow-feeling not to label him? By empathy to feel they are the members one of another, a recognition of basic humanity which can then accept and glory in differences without divisiveness? How prevent teachers from grooming those pupils for double failure, academic and cultural? The fact that a school is labelled 'comprehensive' need make little difference. On the contrary, as Dr Julienne Ford's 1969 research shows and as Dennis Marsden underlines, a *meritocratic comprehensive* with its policy of rigid streaming and early specialization, concentrating its major resources on the so-called academic high-flyers, does not lead to greater development of talent, to greater equality of opportunity for those with equal talent, to widening occupational horizons and raising occupational aspirations, to increasing social contact across class boundaries.[7] In short, such a school can be as rejective as streamed grammar and secondary moderns in the bipartite system and does not lessen the present inbuilt social discrimination against working-class pupils. So Robbins's 'large reservoirs of untapped ability' are in such schools still largely untapped and will remain so until they alter their ethic from a competitive and acquisitive one to a co-operative and community one, recognize that all cultures are relative and have validity, and reshape their education to put it into practice. The fact that our comprehensive schools as a whole, deprived of the very ablest pupils though most of them still are, are keeping in one-eighth more pupils beyond the compulsory leaving age than the bipartite system is proof of their rapidly increasing movement towards true comprehensiveness.

The specialists in comparative education at the Päadagogisches Zentrum in West Berlin call meritocratic streamed comprehensive schools *additive*. They distinguish these very carefully from the five true unstreamed comprehensives which they have since 1965 set up in Berlin, which they call *integrated*, and which they founded to help in the democratization of their society and the pursuit of the greatest possible equality of educational opportunity for all. They have been influenced by our own integrated comprehensives, and the ethic the most famous of theirs, the Martin-Buber-Schule, and the others adhere to is that of co-operation and community.[8]

What practical procedures and principles ought an integrated comprehensive to adopt to implement its ethic of co-operation and community and cultural relativity? Or – to put it in the narrower form of our present problem – to give the kind of education to all pupils upon which the extra fifth year can be successfully built and far more than at present high-ability working-class pupils voluntarily stay on afterwards?

Ideally, during the first three years – already, in fact, done in some schools – the pupils should be taught for as many subjects as possible in mixed-ability groups. This is to prevent self-fulfilling assumptions being made about them – those are A's, those B's, and so on.

Special individual and co-operative small-group teaching-learning patterns have to be developed to teach mixed-ability groups successfully. The abler must be fully stretched and doing work of the quality they would be doing in a good grammar school, the least able developing and progressing at least as well as in an efficient remedial class in a good secondary modern. A great deal by practising teachers on the necessary techniques is fortunately already in print.[9] As in any streamed class, some subjects are more difficult to teach than others. For these *setting*, i.e. grouping according to the ability shown in that particular subject, is often used. This is not to say that one wishes to set for these subjects. It is rather a practical recognition of where one stands and what one feels one can cope with in the present state of one's knowledge, experience and expertise. Many of our integrated schools set only for mathematics, science and modern languages; some postpone this until well on in the third year, then only taking out from each group of, say, ninety pupils, one aptitude set of thirty plus, leaving the other two undifferentiated.

An integrated school, then, to keep the position as flexible and open-ended as possible, so that the pupil can without prejudice find his own levels as he goes up through the school, finally selecting himself for the course he will follow from the fourth year on, should aim at doing as little setting as possible during the first three years. The advances of modern educational technology, and the structured teaching materials that are being or will be available from publishers – some initiated by such bodies as the Schools Council and the various Nuffield Projects Teams – will enable them soon to achieve this aim.

Such flexible and open-ended teaching is a basic way of embodying the values of an integrated accepting school, academically and culturally. The other values which are an essential part of its ethic I can briefly sum up as if to a first-year pupil, though the essential message will remain as relevant to him in the rest of his school life, including the extra fifth year and thereafter. It's this:

We respect you equally and are concerned for you equally, regardless of who or what you are. We haven't put you into streams, labelled you A, B, C, D, because we're *optimistic* about you. We're going to teach you as well as we know how: you'll have your fair share of the best teachers and the best equipment. If you work hard and steadily, who knows what you can achieve? We don't believe you are donkeys who need perpetual carrots to make you go. So we are not going to give you marks. We'll grade you later on so that you know where you stand in the examination stakes, we'll tell you what sort of a chance we think you have of passing, but the true reward and the greatest personal development comes from doing your best to make steady progress. Who have you got to beat here? Nobody. Except yourself. Here we compare ourselves only with our best selves. So we don't have competitive mark-lists, prizes and prize-days. We believe you can all be successful at so many things, and each brings its own reward. We don't publish our examination results either, though we're proud of them. This would be to ask for public recognition of only one aspect of our work and thus to seem to give it too much importance. The challenge lies in trying the examination, the reward in facing it and, where possible, passing. Whether we like it or not, if you want certain jobs, the first step is to get certain examinations. But passing examinations is only one kind of success. There are so many other things you can succeed at. Live a full and happy life here – there's so much to do – and there's a good chance, given average luck, that you'll lead a full and happy life later on.

Certain things are implicit in this and need bringing out. Only if all a pupil's educational activities, academic and cultural, are valued, and seen to be valued, will he who would have left at 15, the so-called 'early leaver', have the right attitude towards the extra year.

Nowhere is it more important than here to abandon mere academicism, with its disproportionate emphasis upon books in learning and its belief that this is the only kind of learning that matters and which therefore deserves praise and recognition.

Similarly, only when the false dichotomies between 'pure and applied', 'liberal and vocational', 'theoretical and practical' and the present inane hierarchy of subjects are abolished, will the potential 'new sixth-former', in a sixth form largely made up of high-ability working-class pupils, feel himself valued enough to stay for further education, and believe firmly enough that what he is being offered is in truth *relevant* to his needs.

Indeed, the very term 'sixth-former', with its implicit and outmoded one-dimensional grammar-school assumptions of the kind referred to above, shouldn't be used. All are simply pupils staying for the sixth year, the seventh, the eighth. The job of the integrated school is to see that whether their objective is to enter a university or to shelter until they are ready to go out into the world, they are equally welcome and gainfully employed. This is a multi-dimensional view of individuals, flexible enough to embrace them in all their infinite variety and richness, and one which is not tied to any particular set of class or quasi-academic assumptions. It can therefore speak to all sorts and conditions of pupils.

Any subject can be made educative or non-educative according to the spirit and manner in which it is taught. This is recognized as tellingly as anywhere in the *School Council's Project Technology* (Bulletin 10). The new sixth will be more responsive to the approach this bulletin typifies than to that embodied in the traditional, pure sixth form, with its public-school echoes of turning out superior and paternalistic gentlemen unsullied by acquaintance with anything of practical use.

The kind of thinking represented by this approach is fortunately also now to be seen, not only in the Certificate of Secondary Education, especially Mode 3, but also in the General Certificate of Education, Ordinary and Advanced Levels. The opportunities this wide and widening gamut of examinations gives of including a much larger spectrum of pupils than hitherto and, just as important, of pupils whose minds work in different ways and whose talents manifest themselves differently, is contributing greatly to the solution of our problem. The next step is to bring the two examinations together. This would kill the present status-differentiation – G.C.E. superior, C.S.E. inferior-which was inevitable and should have been foreseen. The importance of the once-for-all situation so common still in G.C.E., and which favours a certain type of mind, often very well coached, could also then be reduced and the main weight and emphasis be placed on course work and continuous assessment, oral as well as written. The movement some examination boards are making to change the nature of the once-for-all test, substituting where appropriate multiple-choice techniques and methods of assessing skills not tested by orthodox examinations, will also help. Most important of all, the pass-fail concept should be done away with as a first step in destroying the one-dimensional pass-fail concept of human ability which it embodies. Only a dwindling minority would not be able to achieve some meaningful success. At the higher levels we need something diagnostically better than the present A level – multi-dimensional, also. For surely also the present dichotomies in tertiary education – Oxbridge first, the Rest always second; Universities first, polytechnics second; the status-madness of the binary system – must soon come to an end.

If such thinking and such measures as I have outlined were adopted, we could create an accepting system of education in which no one was groomed for double failure. Yet what of the early leavers? As they are now? And how can the non-examination pupils of the future, however their numbers dwindle, not feel they are failures? Let me suggest some answers based upon what's being done at my own school.

In this work, above all else, teachers should accept, respect and be concerned for their pupils, and maturely committed to them. They should on the grounds of their own experience believe and make explicit that getting on doesn't necessarily mean rising up, that success has many faces, that there are as many roads to fulfilment and happiness as there are human beings. But all must be good roads: true happiness springs only from virtue.

The course itself, which we call the Core Course, should be organized on a thematic and not a subject basis. Here is where an interdisciplinary approach pays off. The themes should be chosen because they are relevant to the pupil: once a good relationship is established, pupils will, if asked, tell you what these are. 'Relevant' here means, in the pupils' words, 'useful for my job, or in my future life'. A good teacher can suggest other themes, and each year they can if necessary be changed. He should in addition be able to justify everything that is done.

The basic team of teachers should be supplemented by subject specialists, but specialists who have volunteered to do the work. Team planning and team teaching are essential.

The closeness of the relationship between the basic team and the pupils, upon which all else hinges, should not be allowed to develop into dependency. The fact that subject specialists also teach them and they are expected to work and behave also for them helps to prevent this. The approach to learning should be multi-dimensional, engaging all the senses, through film, film-strip, pictures, tape, records, TV and radio, newspapers, and above all *things* themselves. The most precious end-product is discussion, but discussion tactfully steered towards using what is learnt in as rational and critical a way as possible, and leading to self and social awareness.

The major themes of our present course are: Your City; Your Home and Family; Your Work; Your World; Your Leisure.

The headings of a sub-section of Your Home and Family entitled Problems of Personal Relationships are: Religious and personal beliefs – death and future life; Moral standards; Social problems – crime, gambling, drugs, promiscuity and V.D.; Boy-and-girl friendships – love and lust; contraceptives. For instance, a full discussion on the latter comes within the context of all the work done on the sub-section and at a time in the course when the relationship between pupils and teachers has been cemented, and is followed by a visit from a member of the Family Planning Association, who in the teacher's presence displays and allows to be examined the whole contraceptive range, and always to mixed groups. Questions follow, the teacher being deliberately used by the F.P.A. member as reference-point and sounding-board: both in our experience are always asked for their opinions and give them personally and sincerely.

Another sub-section of the same theme sets out to arrive at a true concept of homelessness. The climax of this is an exhibition in which *Shelter* leaflets, newspaper and magazine cuttings, sketches, photographs taken by pupils, calculations of rents and budgets, local human-interest stories, and more abstract essays all feature. The quality of the written work shows the very real involvement and effort to be literate the pupils make.

Other features of the Core Course deserve mention. An average of two out-of-school visits a week take place – two-thirds to the kinds of places most of these pupils are likely to find work in, e.g. shops, factories, small businesses, and one-third to other places to widen their knowledge of how people in their own city earn a living. This is supported by fortnightly talks from outside speakers. When the extra year comes, this should be further supplemented by opportunities for varied work-experience, and the Government, trade unions, and L.E.A.s should begin to plan for this now.

Outside the main scheme, early leavers can choose to do art, music, games, domestic studies and technical studies. The pressure on the specialist rooms is always great, and when all such pupils are with us for the extra year more work-rooms and workshops which can be linked to their work-experience and where they can learn by further doing will be necessary.

Finally, I'd like to say something about the School and Social Service Programme that the Core Course carries out. Here is a list of some of the jobs they volunteer for and do: weekly visits to from fifty to sixty old age pensioners (in pairs, doing shopping, house-cleaning, digging gardens, chopping firewood, and – most important – being company); visiting and entertaining in school members of a physically handicapped centre; nursery school helpers (four girls each week in two nurseries); infant school clinic duty (escorts for infants at telephoned request of headmistresses); old people's club helpers (about a dozen each Tuesday afternoon help to entertain and feed the 100 members of the David Lister Old People's Club); reporters and sub-editors, house weekly newspaper; running the school tuck-shop; supervising the lost property (kept in one of their classrooms and available twice daily, 1–1.15 and 4–4.15 p.m.); servicing the drinks machines; doing the house refreshments at parents' evenings; packing and distributing the Harvest Festival and Christmas gifts to our old people; cleaning and helping to service the school expeditions' bus.

Each house runs its own social service programme, but none on the scale of the Core Course. Service by itself is no substitute for a true sense of community, of a shared and common humanity. Added to it, though, as it is in an integrated accepting school, it can play a fundamental part in the making of persons.

REFERENCES

1 Douglas, J. W. B., Ross, J. M., and Simpson, H. R., *All Our Future*, London: Peter Davies, 1968.

2 Himmelweit, Hilde T., and Swift, Betty, 'A Model for the Understanding of School as a Socializing Agent', in Mussen, P., Langer, J., Covington, M. (eds.), *Trends and Issues in Developmental Psychology*, New York: Rinehart Winston, 1969.

3 Jackson, Brian, *Streaming: an Education System in Miniature*, London: Routledge & Kegan Paul, 1964.

4 Young, Michael, *The Rise of the Meritocracy*, London: Thames & Hudson, 1958, and Penguin Books, 1968.

5 Rowe, Albert, 'The Case against Streaming', in *Unstreaming in the*

Comprehensive School, Where?, Supplement 12, Cambridge: Advisory Centre for Education, 1968.

6 Rowe, Albert, 'Human Beings, Class and Education', in Rubinstein, David, and Stoneman, Colin (eds.), *Education for Democracy*, London: Penguin Books, 1970.

7 Ford, Julienne, *Social Class and the Comprehensive School*, London: Routledge & Kegan Paul, 1969.

8 Lohmann, Joachim, and Magdeburg, Horst, *Gesamptschulen Informationsdienst*, Berlin: Pädagogisches Zentrum, S.69, 1968.

9 E.g. ed. Simon, Brian, *Forum for the Discussion of New Trends in Education*, selected volumes, 86 Headland Road, Evington, Leicester. Hoyles, E. M., 'Vauxhall Manor School, London', *Institute of Education Bulletin*, Spring Term, 1967. Eds. McAlhone, Beryl, and Rowe, Albert, *Unstreaming in the Comprehensive School*, op. cit.

7 Preparations for changes in the curriculum

Denis Lawton

Introduction

Nearly all industrial societies have committed themselves to a policy of universal secondary education, but none has yet completely solved the problem of what to include in this universal programme. Additionally, most countries are pressing ahead with proposals for extending the period of compulsory education without waiting for a satisfactory answer to be given to this problem. The reasons for the widespread uncertainty are that the problems involved in providing secondary education for all are extremely complex.

In this country it is sometimes said that the struggle is between the *elitists* and the egalitarians, but this is really a vast over-simplification. The recent Black Paper has made very clear that there are many kinds of *elitists*; similarly, among those who think of themselves (or who are thought of) as egalitarians there is no total agreement on policy. For example, one of the goals of compulsory education is universal literacy, and most educationists as well as most of the population would agree on this as a goal. But even at this level there is no total agreement. At least one Professor of Education, Geoffrey Bantock, does not hold this opinion. In his book, *Culture, Industrialization and Society*, he quotes with approval the statement made by D. H. Lawrence that 'The great mass of humanity should never learn to read and write – never'. Bantock justifies his support of Lawrence in this respect by saying the vast majority of the population have a culture which is non-literary in its origins. This folk-culture has been partly destroyed by the process of industrialization, but, according to Bantock, the urban proletariat are still not capable of benefiting from the 'high culture'. He goes on to support his opinion by describing some of the failures of popular education. Bantock is certainly right in claiming that no one has solved the problem of what to include in the curriculum for the majority of the secondary-school population – let alone how to teach this. His solution is, however, a non-answer, and seems to fall into the trap of saying that if we cannot go back to merry England, where the peasants were happy and creative in their own simple way, at least let us stay where we are and avoid slipping further down the slope towards egalitarianism. This is an extreme view of a curriculum, or, rather, a non-curriculum, for secondary education, but a number of people would share the opinion that it is a waste of time trying to *educate* 'the masses': 'Instruct them in useful skills by all means,' they might say, 'but be realistic and don't try to aim too high!' This is the implication contained in many unsolicited testimonials for secondary modern schools: for example, one from Quintin Hogg:

> I can assure Hon. Members opposite that if they would go to study what is now being done in good secondary modern schools, they would not find a lot of pupils biting their nails in frustration because they had failed the 11 plus. The pleasant noise of banging metal and sawing wood would greet their ears and a smell of cooking with rather expensive equipment would come out of the front door to greet them. They would find that these boys and girls were getting an education tailor-made to their desires, their bents and their requirements. (*Hansard*, 21 January 1965, p. 424, quoted in J. D. Koerner 1968).

Such advocates of secondary education might want equality of educational opportunity (weakly defined) so that bright children get a chance of advancement, but they would not really want 'education' in its true sense for all pupils, or they might not think it a realistic goal.

At the other extreme we have those who deny innate ability altogether. According to them, everything is due to environment. Therefore all the school has to do is to provide an enriched or compensatory environment and all children would educate themselves. Somewhere in between these two extremes there are those who recognize the existence of innate differences, but who suggest that they can be greatly modified by environmental factors, and who say if you believe in equality and democracy you must provide an opportunity for *every* child to achieve a satisfactory basic minimum education and at the same time allow plenty of opportunity for every child to go on as far beyond that basic minimum as he or she is capable. The argument about the raising of the school leaving age is really a question about 'Can we do this for *most* children by the age of 15?' There is also a less open question: 'Is it worth trying to do this for *all* children?'

Changes in the curriculum and other kinds of preparations made for the raising of the school leaving age must be seen against this kind of lack of consensus about the aims and objectives of secondary education. Another, very different, kind of *elitist* attack on our present provision of secondary education might best be represented by the American educationist, J. D. Koerner, who dislikes the British emphasis on equality of opportunity (especially comprehensive schools), but also criticizes the low level of education which we seem to have in mind for the majority of our secondary-school pupils. Koerner gives us a very perceptive analysis of a situation in which teachers and educationists generally lack clarity about what they think secondary education is for. At the end of his book, Koerner sets out a series of alternative goals: education as an instrument of social change; as an arm of the Welfare State to be a child-minding institute; schools as job-training centres; or schools which will initiate pupils into the basic subjects of human knowledge. His analysis is that most schools seem to be going in the direction of non-academic life-adjustment courses or vocational training rather than true education. His advice would be to make our pupils work harder, raise their levels of aspiration and introduce them to real knowledge. This is a perceptive analysis, but seems to confuse the issue by implying that this can be achieved without our having to modify the present highly selective system. Most sociologists would see the kind of curriculum reform that Koerner wants as an inextricable part of a general reform of secondary education.

A point of view in some ways similar to that of Koerner, but expressed cogently in philosophical terms, has been put forward by Professor P. H. Hirst. Hirst agrees that education is primarily concerned with the transmission of knowledge, and that knowledge consists of a number (seven or eight) of distinct and autonomous forms of knowledge. Hirst's major contribution to the raising of the school leaving age issue is his insistence that if we accept an egalitarian view of education, and if we are really committed to equality of educational opportunity, then it follows that an attempt must be made to initiate *all* pupils into forms of knowledge and understanding. Some will undoubtedly achieve greater understanding than others, but all pupils must be led towards the same objectives. The method of teaching pupils may be different according to their level of ability or aspiration, but the forms of knowledge which are the educational objectives must of necessity be the same for all pupils.

This would seem to be a strong argument against some of the so-called Newsom Courses which are referred to later in this chapter, but it should not be seen as an argument in favour of extending the traditional grammar-school curriculum to all pupils of all abilities (which was the implication of the Koerner argument). There is no great degree of correspondence between the traditional grammar-school curriculum and Hirst's seven forms of knowledge. If Hirst is right, therefore, there is a need for all secondary schools to re-think their total curricula.

This range of opinions regarding the 'problems' connected with raising the school leaving age makes it necessary to analyse very carefully both the background to the problem and the present situation before attempting to evaluate some of the proposals which have been put forward for a curriculum for the final year at school. That is, we must try to clarify the issue in question before pronouncing on the kind of courses which some may want to provide.

What are the social pressures behind the movement to raise the school leaving age? I have suggested elsewhere (Lawton, 1968) that the social pressures most powerfully exerting an influence on schools and school systems can best be divided under the three headings of Economic, Ideological (the move from an *elitist* towards an egalitarian society) and Secular/Rational (the move away from Christian values and ways of thinking to more secular/rational views).

The Economic Pressures

In relation to this particular issue of the raising of the school leaving age, the economic argument is probably the weakest of the three. It is, of course, true that as the process of industrialization continues, and as such factors as automation become more widespread, there is a declining demand for unskilled and semi-skilled manpower and a corresponding increase in demand for more skilled workers of many kinds. It has been argued that the need is not only to produce technicians rather than operatives, which will involve a general raising of levels of achievement, but also to produce workers who are more flexible, who have been taught general principles rather than specific skills, so that they can readily abandon jobs which become redundant and obsolete and apply themselves to new industrial skills and techniques.

All of this would seem to be beyond question, but it is not in itself an entirely convincing argument for raising the school leaving age. It could be argued that from a purely economic point of view it would be more efficient to change the kind of teaching that pupils receive up to the age of 15 and to make even greater changes to the kind of training in apprenticeship, etc., that youngsters now receive having left school – less of the 'sitting next to Nelly' kind of practice, but more general technical education, including maths and science. In addition, it would be necessary to expand the training which young people now receive (only 40% of 15-year-old male leavers now enter apprenticeship schemes of any kind). From an economic point of view this alternative proposal might be theoretically desirable; whether it is a practical possibility, given existing resources for industrial training, is another matter. The evidence provided by the extremely disappointing results so far of the Industrial Training Act might make one more optimistic that schools could adapt to change more effectively than industry.

Ideological Pressures

One of the major preoccupations of sociologists since the war has been to document the difference between the *ideal* of equality of educational opportunity implied in the 1944 Act and the *reality* of what actually happens in schools. This gap between the opportunities available to middle-class pupils as compared with the children of manual workers has been shown to exist at all levels from the age of 5 to university entrance, and the problem could perhaps best be summed up in the words of the *Crowther Report*, which suggested that the education received by the majority of the population was 'inadequate both in its quality and in its duration'. This is an important point of view, since it emphasizes that *two* changes are necessary if the school leaving age is raised – *quality* and duration. Simply to extend the duration without improving quality might be worse than useless. This warning was uttered in 1965 by Lionel Elvin: 'There are experiments in some schools, often showing enterprise and imagination. But by and large we have not thought this problem out, and we have not deliberately trained teachers to do it. If the higher school leaving age comes into effect before we have done so the result will be not merely wasteful, but disastrous.'

There is, however, another interesting gap which is as important as the social-class gap referred to in the paragraph above. This is the gap between the attitude of official Reports like Crowther and Newsom and the views of those at local level who are responsible for making changes. Perhaps this point can best be made by historical reference: the ideological contrast between mid-nineteenth century and mid-twentieth century is a sharp one. The nineteenth-century view of society was still unself-consciously hierarchical and *elitist* rather than democratic; the great nineteenth-century Commissions and Enquiries on education, such as the Newcastle Commission or the Taunton Commission, saw nothing wrong with the notion of different kinds of school, different qualities of education with quite different curricula to correspond to the different social classes in society. Today we have by no means achieved equality, but it is now the official policy established by the 1944 Act, and has even been interpreted by Plowden as the need for *positive* discrimination. My point here is that although this is now official policy, and although few people publicly quarrel with the principle, in practice many people concerned with education – for example, teachers, head teachers, administrators, local government officials and elected representatives – only pay lip service to the principle, and beneath the surface may still retain an *elitist* attitude on questions of educational provision. This may be expressed in a reluctance to provide new school buildings in slum areas or to provide recreational facilities for the youth service at anything like the scale thought to be minimal for universities and colleges of education, or, perhaps most importantly of all, it shows itself at secondary level in a reluctance to think of a curriculum which would be real education rather than mere containment.

A related point is that education for working-class so-called non-academic 14–15-year-olds is often seen as a means of education for citizenship or training for democracy. The danger here is that unless this objective is seen as part of a programme of *education* (i.e. real understanding of the problems, which would necessitate an initiation into the social sciences, such as economics, political science, sociology), a civic approach to secondary education becomes no more than indoctrination or manipulation.

On the other hand, a well-reasoned argument in favour of raising the school leaving age could be based partly on the 'explosion of knowledge' view, and partly on a sociological view connected with the failure of the policy of parity of esteem. The 'explosion of knowledge' view would simply say that if we really want pupils to understand the world in which they live in a mathematical way, a scientific way, etc., then this simply cannot be done by the age of 16 – especially when much of the thinking required must be of an abstract nature, probably beyond the level of many 14–15-year-olds.

The second argument, regarding the failure of parity of prestige in secondary education, would link raising the school leaving age to the more general problems of secondary education and recommendations for comprehensive schools. Olive Banks, in her book, *Parity and Prestige in English Secondary Education* (1955), made the point very clearly that in a society which accords differential prestige to the products of two different kinds of school, then automatically the schools themselves are accorded different kinds of esteem. This is part of the argument for comprehensive school systems, and it would also apply to those pupils aged 15 to 16 who in the past would not have been classified as academic: if we accept the principle of equality, not only must they have the same kind of curriculum, but they must also have an adequate amount of time to mature and master the curriculum. This would also relate to the Crowther statement regarding greater *quality* as well as duration.

So far the argument has been idealistic and theoretical rather than practical. This is inevitable: if we believe in equality of opportunity, then it is the task of teachers not to waste time arguing 'when' or 'whether', but to find out *how* to achieve this goal. There is no reason to think that this kind of education is beyond the capacity of the majority of the population. This view has been accepted in an unquestioning way for far too long.

The Secular/Rational Pressure

In his contribution to *Schools Council Working Paper*, No. 12, Professor Sprott connected the growth of rationality with concern for people (which I have considered above separately as part of the ideological change). I would agree that these two aspects of modern life are closely connected, but not that they are identical, and I would prefer to analyse them separately. I would also want to stress the change from a religious to a more secular society. For good or ill, people are less influenced by Christian doctrine, and many people have suggested that it is important that a rational basis for morality be provided in schools. The really important change in objectives in education here is that we can no longer believe it sufficient for young people to be obedient and to conform to laws and rules; if they conform they must do so for the right reasons (i.e. rational ones), and occasionally we might even approve of their non-conformity if this is also based on rational decisions. Part of the difficulty of living in a pluralist society is precisely that a number of choices have to be made regarding behaviour in politics or morals and that, even if religious issues are at stake, decisions should be taken on rational lines.

If one important objective in secondary education is to acquire a rational basis for moral decision-making, then this is quite clearly a powerful argument for keeping pupils at school until they have reached the stage of maturation which will make this kind of learning easier or even possible. The work of Piaget, Kohlberg and others suggests that 15 is a dangerously early leaving age for many young people in this respect.

Once again, however, it must be stressed that this is not simply a question of maturation. There is no reason to believe that rational thinking will simply develop with increasing age; it must be taught. This ought to give us a considerable help in deciding the content of the curriculum for the 15–16-year-old pupils (see later references to the work of Wilson, McPhail and Stenhouse).

With that general background in mind, we might now examine in some detail some of the specific suggestions that have been made for a programme for the school-leavers.

The *Crowther Report* was of course not only concerned with 15-plus leavers, It was also concerned with sixth forms of grammar schools. The 'leavers' were divided into two groups by the *Crowther Report*: the minority who would proceed to some form of further education, and the majority who would not. The Crowther recommendation was that the school leaving age should be raised from 15 to 16, and that the extra year should be at school. Presumably members of the Committee were thinking that the curriculum for the extra year should resemble the ideal four strands that they envisaged as the Further Education curriculum: (1) to help young people find their way about the world; (2) moral values; (3) education for leisure; and (4) education in a narrow sense – vocational and intellectual. In retrospect, perhaps the most striking fact about Crowther is the complacent attitude towards the grammar-school curriculum, especially the sixth form curriculum, which is more specialized than anywhere else in the world. The opportunity for making a significant contribution to curriculum development was sadly missed on this occasion.

The *Newsom Report* took the analysis of 'secondary education for all' one stage further by widening the definition of secondary education. It suggested that so-called extra-curricular activities should be considered an essential part of school. To enable these to be incorporated, they suggested an extension of the school day. This might be regarded as a very important reform, but it has in fact received very little support from teachers or administrators.

As a document on the curriculum suitable for *Half Our Future*, the Report is a peculiar mixture of optimism and traditional stereotyped thinking. On the one hand, the Committee recommends that all pupils should have more and better science teaching, and should have the opportunity of learning a foreign language (probably the least important aspect of the high-prestige grammar-school curriculum); they also had some extremely useful and sensible suggestions to make on English teaching, as well as on 'practical subjects'; on the other hand, whilst recognizing the need for young people to understand their own society, the remedy suggested seemed to be a re-vamped version of history, geography and R.I. rather than any new ideas about incorporating the social sciences. The greatest shortcoming of the *Newsom Report* was, however, that it lent itself to being interpreted as an argument in favour of the outward-looking, life-adjustment courses which I have criticized earlier in this chapter. The fact that so many schools have simply opted for 'Newsom Courses' for non-academic 'Newsom' children is in itself a condemnation of the fact that the *Report* did not take a more positive line on a curriculum, not for 'Half Our Future', but for 'All Our Future'.

Schools Council Working Paper No. 2, *Raising the School Leaving Age: A Co-operative Programme of Research and Development*, is in many respects a much more revolutionary document than either Crowther or Newsom. *Working Paper*, No. 2, suggests that

> The possibility of helping the pupils who are the concern of this paper to enter the world of ideas, to use powers of reason and to acquire even the beginnings of mature judgment, may seem to contradict the experience of many teachers. Indeed, it may carry an almost revolutionary ring to some, and this accounts for the tentative character of many of the ideas put forward in this Working Paper. It is often said that these pupils are not interested in ideas; they cannot handle abstractions; they cannot verbalize; they make choices by comparing immediate satisfactions; they are only interested in people and

concrete situations. It is just these assumptions which the
raising of the school leaving age gives all in the sphere of
secondary education the opportunity to challenge. For the more
able pupils, now staying on voluntarily in increasing numbers,
the fifth year has revealed powers which many did not suspect.
When, for some 60% of the pupils, schooling stops often
before the fourth year is out, and before a sufficient maturity
is reached, possibilities for development may be undiscovered.
This is the basic assumption which the *Newsom Report* asks us
to make when it calls for a change of heart in our attitudes
towards the slower learners. In thinking about what is
desirable, and practicable, in developing new curricula and
courses for the young school-leaver, the standpoint of this
Working Paper is thus that some existing assumptions, though
soundly based on current experience, may be invalid in the
situation which would follow the raising of the school leaving
age. There is evidence from Further and Adult Education,
and from the experience of those few schools which have
successfully held appreciable numbers of the less able pupils
for a fifth year of secondary education, that doors can be
thrown open where current experience of a four-year course
might suggest that they must remain closed. There is also
evidence from primary education that practically all pupils
can acquire insights into abstract ideas, and a capacity to work
with them (particularly by oral means), if doors are opened
through the use of teaching methods which build on the pupils'
present experience and supply new forms of experience which
help them to discover for themselves the powers of their own
minds.

The *Working Paper* did not, however, simply express pious hopes
about what might be achieved. It went on to make positive suggestions about what the curriculum should include. It suggested that
the curriculum should possess organic unity, and that the organizing
principle most likely to provide a sound basis for development was
the study of man, and of human society, human needs and purposes.

The suggestion was that subjects like English, geography,
history and religious education which had previously been studied
in isolation might now be combined into a humanities course which
would deal with men and women in relation to their environment,
their communities and their own self-knowledge. This did not
appear to be a recommendation for any kind of life-adjustment

course, but rather for bringing economics, sociology, psychology, anthropology, etc., to bear on problems of the modern world. The complexity of the task here was recognized and it was therefore decided that the Council would offer its support to a feasibility study financed and organized by the Nuffield Foundation. The study was designed to discover how far it would be possible to offer the schools organized forms of help in tackling the problems of new humanities courses. The terms of reference given for the feasibility study were:

> The team should assume that the Headmaster of a comprehensive school (which draws boys and girls from both town and country areas) has asked for help. He is concerned about the last year or two of work for those who do not take O level, and is particularly aware that some of his problems will grow more acute in five years' time when the school leaving age is raised. His school is adequately equipped with modern aids, and (more important) has members of staff in the departments of English, R.I., history and geography who would be prepared to co-operate in a new scheme which is more relevant than present courses to the needs and aspirations of pupils of average and below-average ability. One-third of the weekly time-table could be made available for this new course; some of those who took the course would attempt C.S.E., but many would not. Several neighbours, including a social scientist, might give help on a part-time basis, and the school is willing to consider flexible arrangements for out-of-school work, including projects and assignments based on other institutions.
>
> The team are asked to advise such a Headmaster whether a curriculum-development group could produce materials that would help these teachers to mount a worthwhile course; they should indicate what form such a course and such materials might take. The main question will concern what attitudes, experiences, skills and knowledge are important in adult life, to society as well as the individual. In their study of this question the team should consider in particular: (*a*) what is likely to be of interest to boys and girls (and therefore conducive to a 'learning experience') during the final years of secondary school? (*b*) what can be discovered from successful courses of this kind that have already been tried out (not only for pupils of this level of ability, but also in sixth forms and further education colleges), apart from the fact that the teachers of them may be especially gifted? (*c*) what can be learnt from

the failures of past attempts in this field, and from justifiable criticisms (by young people themselves, employers or others) of what the schools now provide?

There were elements of ambiguity in this brief, but much of the *Working Paper* does contain sound educational ideas. Unfortunately, the translation of the ideals of *Working Paper*, No. 2, into reality in the form of *Working Paper*, No. 11, is much less satisfactory. This paper, *Society and the Young School Leaver*, has been criticized so severely that the tendency now is to ignore it completely or to assume that it has been completely superseded. There is a great deal of poorly-thought-out material in the paper (much of it of the life-adjustment kind), but it is not completely without merit. For example, one of the four suggestions on how an area of inquiry might be developed (in the Appendix) is much superior to the other three. The main criticism has been that such projects as the 97 'bus are really 'soft options' rather than alternative approaches to acquiring forms of knowledge. John White, for example, in an article in *New Society*, criticized such approaches, not only because they did not clearly have any worthwhile knowledge content, but also because they appeared to him to be forms of indoctrination – encouraging young working-class pupils to accept their lot in life rather than to rebel against them. Many other educationists were equally unhappy about the kind of inter-disciplinary work of a low intellectual level suggested in *Working Paper*, No. 11; and the follow-up study financed by Nuffield and Schools Council directed by Lawrence Stenhouse has taken a very different line of approach to that set out in the *Working Paper*, No. 11. The view adopted by Lawrence Stenhouse and his team working on the Humanities Curriculum Project will be discussed in some detail below.

Out of the rather confusing array of opinions, recommendations and suggestions contained in the above official and semi-official documents regarding the raising of the school leaving age, four main curricular problems emerge in a fairly unambiguous way:

1 *Vocational requirements of an extended course:* the need to present more opportunities to more pupils to acquire greater knowledge and understanding, especially of science and technology.
2 *Social:* to extend pupils' ability to understand the political, economic and sociological issues of their own and other societies.
3 *Moral:* to reach a rational basis for moral decision-making.
4 *Recreational:* to equip all pupils with the means of enjoying the non-vocational aspects of adult life, and also to regard

Preparations for changes in the curriculum 109

education as something which does not end at 15 or 16, but which should continue throughout life.

To achieve all of this would be a very tall order indeed, but a number of preparations have been made to incorporate at least some of these goals or objectives into the curriculum. These will be described in the next section.

Some of the preparations have been made on a one-year or two-year basis, others – more realistically – represent a tendency to re-think the curriculum for the whole secondary-school age-range, and are set out as from eleven to sixteen projects. It should perhaps be stressed that this is not an exhaustive list, but only a few significant examples:

1   *Vocational* (in the sense of acquiring real knowledge about science and technology rather than job training in the sense condemned by Koerner above).

a   Mathematics for the Majority: a Schools Council Secondary School Mathematics Project. Directed by Philip Floyd, University of Exeter.

This project aims to meet the mathematical needs of pupils of average and below-average ability aged 13 to 16. It is concerned with the production, trial and dissemination of teaching materials, presented mainly through a series of guides for teachers. The aims of the project team are:

1   To provide pupils with experience of mathematical situations, to encourage powers of judgment and the exercise of imagination.
2   To give pupils some understanding of the mathematical concepts which underlie the numeracy required for everyday affairs.
3   To remove barriers isolating mathematics from other areas of the curriculum and other interests of the pupils.
4   To enable pupils to appreciate in some measure the order and pattern of their environment.

The secondary mathematics project will not be completed until 1973, but before the school leaving age is raised a number of pilot schools will have reported back, and materials and ideas will be available to schools throughout the country. It is as yet too early to make any assessment about the final results of the project: it has been received with enthusiasm by many teachers but detailed results are not yet available. Perhaps even more important than the result, however, is the aim. The stated objectives of the project clearly set out the principle of teaching real mathematical knowledge by new methods. It is not a

'watered-down' sort of mathematics designed for the less able to play with; it is a genuine form of knowledge and understanding.
b The Applied Science and Technology Project (Schools Council Project Technology). Directed by Mr G. B. Harrison, Loughborough College of Education.

The goal of this project is not to introduce technology as a new subject on the time-table, but to encourage schools to foster an understanding of technology and to encourage a creative attitude towards it. The overall objectives of the project are expressed as: 'To help all children to get to grips with technology as a major influence in our society and, as a result, to help more of them to lead effective and satisfying lives.'

This is perhaps a very good example of a merging of the educational needs of individual pupils with the economic needs of society. *Schools Council Working Paper*, No. 18, specifies the four manpower needs that were the concern of the project in the following way:

1 A sufficient proportion of able pupils choosing scientific and technological careers.
2 An adequate supply of candidates to train as skilled technicians.
3 Administrators and managers with sufficient technical and scientific understanding and knowledge.
4 A working population more prepared and able to learn new skills as the older ones become obsolete with advances in science and technology.

These are clearly seen as manpower needs, but they are not in any way in conflict with educational objectives. 'The first of these manpower objectives is more likely to be achieved if pupils receive a longer period of broad education and if this reflects better the fundamental interaction between disciplines.'

Sixty schools were intially studied at the pilot stage, some based on technical or handicraft departments, others based on science departments, still more operating on a basis of interdepartmental co-operation. One very encouraging feature of the work is the participation of girls in the pilot programmes.

This project is not, of course, designed exclusively for the raising of the school leaving age, but it does have clear relevance to it.

c Science for the Young School-leavers. The Nuffield Science Teaching Project. Directed by Mrs. H. Misselbrook, Chelsea College, Centre for Science Education.

Preparations for changes in the curriculum

This programme is specifically concerned with pupils of average and below average ability aged 13 to 16. The project sets out with the purpose of putting right one of the criticisms made of school science in the *Newsom Report*: 'Too much of the tradition of science teaching is of the nature of confirming foregone conclusions. It is a kind of anti-science, damaging to the lively mind, maybe, but deadly to the not so clever' (para. 423).

The answer, however, was seen not in terms of any kind of interest-based project, but carefully structured experimentation: 'Pupils who are not high-flyers will need considerable help in posing the questions to be asked if their inquiries are to meet with adequate success. This means, for example, that the use of open-ended experiments will probably need to be carefully regulated if confusion and depression from an apparent lack of clear progress and achievement are to be avoided.'

The project team spent a good deal of time on consultation and discussion of the ideal curriculum and eventually selected eight themes, and have indicated the principle ideas and areas of knowledge with which these themes are concerned. The eight themes are:

1 Inter-dependence of living things
2 Continuity of life
3 Biology of man
4 Harnessing energy
5 Extension of sense-perception
6 Movement
7 Using materials
8 The earth and its place in the universe

I, II, III *Social, Moral and Recreational* (the non-vocational aspects of the demand for the raising of the school leaving age).

a The Nuffield Foundation and Schools Council Humanities Curriculum Project. Directed by Lawrence Stenhouse, Philippa Fawcett College, Streatham.

Some reference has already been made to this project, which is probably the most ambitious and highly organized research specifically designed to cope with problems of raising the school leaving age. It should be stressed, however, that the materials referred to below are not necessarily limited to 'average or below-average pupils'. The project refers back to the para. 321 of the Newsom Report in explaining the purpose of the team: 'To set a class to study a carefully defined problem in human conduct and human relations into which boys and girls can project themselves and work out the various implications of different courses of action – this is realistic teaching.'

An introductory leaflet about the project also refers back to *Schools Council Working Paper*, No. 2 (*Working Paper*, No. 11, is discreetly ignored): 'The problem is to give every man some access to a complex cultural inheritance, some hold on his personal life and on his relationships with the various communities to which he belongs, some extension of his understanding of, and sensitivity towards, other human beings. The aim is to forward understanding, discrimination and judgment in the human field.'

The way in which the team is tackling this very interesting but very difficult task is to try to develop pupils' understanding of a number of 'controversial areas of universal human concern'. The controversial issues are approached through a technique of discussion which:

> enables the pupils to take responsibility for their own learning and which protects them from the bias of the teacher; the teacher acts as an impartial and neutral chairman in handling controversial value issues with the group. The pupil's understanding of the issues is given substance and extended in a consideration of a range of 'evidence' which is fed into the discussion.

The materials are designed for the 14–16-year-old age-group (of average and below-average ability without serious reading difficulties). In addition to printed materials there are audio tapes of original material, some of which also appear in printed form. Experimental materials have been tried out in thirty-two pilot schools as well as a number of other educational establishments. Extensive evaluation has been carried out by an independent evaluation officer (Barry MacDonald).

By the time the raising of the school leaving age is effected, materials published by Heinemann Educational Books Ltd. should be on sale to schools wishing to join the experiment. Some training is, however, necessary for teachers.

Nine areas have been selected for experimental study:
1 War and society.
2 Education.
3 The family.
4 Relations between the sexes.

5 Poverty.
6 People and work.
7 Law and order.
8 Living in cities.
9 Race.

Collections of materials will probably be published in the order given above.

An interesting feature of this project is that a complementary Roman Catholic project directed by Mr Tony Higgins at St Mary's College, Strawberry Hill, Twickenham, is investigating the implications of the project for Catholic schools.

b Schools Council Integrated Studies Project.
Director, Mr Bolam, Keele University.

This is a four-year project (1967–71) to examine how broad an application the humanities as a whole can have to the needs of secondary-school pupils, and to explore the possible value and means of integrating various subjects in this field. Materials will be produced and tested in 250 schools. This is not designed specifically for the average and below-average pupils aged 14 to 16, but is designed for the whole of the secondary-school age-range and ability-range.

c The Farmington Trust Research Unit on Moral Education.
Directed by John Wilson at Oxford.

The research unit was set up in October 1965 to conduct research on the topic of moral education. Apart from the Director, who is a philosopher, the unit has two Research Fellows, Norman Williams, a psychologist, and Barry Sugarman, who is a sociologist. The work is expected to continue for at least ten years. The first publication of the Farmington Trust is the work of this research unit, and is a book with the title *Introduction to Moral Education*, published by Penguin Books. This does not set out to provide a curriculum on moral education for secondary-school-leavers, but it does contain a wealth of very important ideas and research, as well as some practical suggestions for the school and for teachers. It should certainly be read by all teachers concerned with the education of 14–16-year-old secondary-school pupils.

d The Schools Council Moral Education Project. Directed by Mr Peter McPhail, University of Oxford Institute of Education.

This research project is quite independent of the Farmington Trust Research Unit, but obviously maintains close contact with it. It is designed to study methods of teaching moral education in schools and providing supporting material for the moral education of young school-leavers.

It would be unfair to give the impression, however, that the only kind of preparations that have been made for the raising of the school leaving age are those national projects supported by the Nuffield Foundation or the Schools Council. One of the tasks assigned to the Schools Council when it was first set up in 1964 was to make preparations for the raising of the school leaving age, and the Council has devoted a great deal of its resources to this end. But many more local projects have also been launched, some of them with great enthusiasm and encouraging results. This kind of curriculum development at grass-roots level was, of course, encouraged by the Schools Council itself, especially in *Working Paper No. 10, Curriculum Development: Teachers' Groups and Centres*, which set out guide-lines for local groups of teachers.

In 1967 a Working Party in Oxfordshire (Chairman, Mr John Hanson, Communications Centre, Gosford Hill School, Kidlington, Oxford) produced a report on 'Non-Academic Education, 14–16'. The Working Party had looked carefully at the *Newsom* recommendations and others, and had designed a curriculum for the 14–16-year-old pupils of average and below-average ability. Some of this curriculum would not be immune to the Koerner criticism about life-adjustment courses quoted above, but it also contains some good materials dealing with 'Man in Society' which would be excellent at any level.

Another, very different, area in which a teachers' centre has been the organizing machinery is in Newham. This may not be typical of teachers' centres, but it is a good example of one. Here the Teachers' Centre's 'leader of curriculum studies' is the extremely energetic Ernest Millington, who keeps in close touch with every secondary school in the area, runs courses and stimulates new thinking. One of his methods is a monthly bulletin, in which he describes interesting new courses outside and inside the borough, especially those which might help pupils learn about their own environment and their own wider society. In this case (and in the case of many other teachers' centres) the organizer sees it as part of his function to keep alive and even to intensify the interest that had originally developed regarded the raising of the school leaving age – this despite the fact that the Government postponed the date. Millington describes this part of his job in these terms:

> In January 1968 the Government postponed the raising of the

school leaving age until 1973. We are now in the era of R.O.S.L.A., contemptuous initials for a cynically deferred education project. Immediately we were faced with the relaxation of tension. Sighs of relief were heard throughout the land. Instead of a universal determination to use the opportunity of a further two years for research and development, in some quarters much of the steam went out of the campaign and some schools lapsed back into apathy, whilst others, not in this authority, reaffirmed the prescription, 'The mixture as before, but with much tougher discipline'. Our job in the Teachers' Centre became more demanding, since the activists of the regular Curriculum Study Group had not only to press on with those aspects of development which would affect the 'reluctant heroes' of our 1973 compulsory extra fifth forms, but struggle throughout our deliberations to maintain the impetus and keep the spirit of excitement and adventure on the move. It gave us what we most urgently needed: time not only to try out new or re-vamped courses, but opportunity to examine experimental work going on throughout the country. It enabled us to take a long and searching look at our objectives and at the underlying psychological and social reasons for the problems. (Extract from *Project*: *The Newham Curriculum Development Bulletin*, No. 6, June 1969).

I would have no hesitation in saying that the development of teachers' centres throughout the country has been one of the most important educational innovations in recent years, not only in regard to the raising of the school leaving age, but for curriculum development as a whole. Unfortunately, there are still some L.E.A.s who seem reluctant to encourage teachers' centres more actively by providing the money and resources to allow them to operate with maximum efficiency.

Conclusion

It would seem to be quite clear from the above description of various kinds of preparation that one-year courses are at best useful temporary measures designed to rectify previous deficiences in the curriculum. For many years to come some schools will have to undertake such salvage operations; in the long run, however, there is no substitute for a re-thinking of the entire secondary school curriculum. The raising of the school leaving age should therefore be seen not as one isolated problem, or a gap to be filled, but as part of a complex of reform measures. The complex will include, for example, how to organize comprehensive schools so that they do not become grammar and secondary schools under a single roof; how to unstream schools and yet preserve opportunities for individual fulfilment at the highest possible level; how to cope with the explosion of knowledge by a policy of adequate coverage, plus a balanced curriculum; how to avoid early specialization; how to organize sixth forms in order to cater for pupils who are not only destined for higher education and for whom A level courses may not be entirely appropriate. This may seem to be an enormous set of problems for schools to solve, but taken together they may even be seen as more manageable than if attempted one at a time. Piecemeal reform almost inevitably results in fragmentation of the curriculum, whereas the indications are that what is really required in English schools in the 1970s is far-sighted, long-term planning which would give the curriculum some kind of logical structure and unity.

REFERENCES

Books and Papers
Banks, O., *Parity and Prestige in English Secondary Education*, London, 1955.
Bantock, G., *Culture, Industrialization and Society*, London, 1968.
Elvin, L., *Education and Contemporary Society*, London, 1965.
Hirst, P. H., 'Liberal Education and the Nature of Knowledge', in *Philosophical Analysis and the Nature of Knowledge*, ed. R. D. Archambault, London, 1965.
Koerner, J. D., *Reform in Education*, London, 1968.
Lawton, D., paper given at N.F.E.R. Conference, *Into Work*, July 1968 (in press).
Sprott, W. J. H., 'Society', in *Schools Council Working Paper*, No. 12.
White, J., 'Curriculum Reform', in *New Society*, 29 April 1968.

Reports, etc.
H.M.S.O., Crowther Report, *15-18*, 1959.
H.M.S.O., Newsom Report, *Half Our Future*, 1963.
H.M.S.O., *Schools Council Working Paper*, No. 2, *Raising the School Leaving Age*, 1965.
H.M.S.O., Ibid., No. 11, *Society and the Young School Leaver*, 1967.
H.M.S.O., Ibid., No. 12, *The Educational Implications of Social and Economic Change*, 1967.
H.M.S.O., Ibid., No. 18, *Technology in Schools*, 1968.

8 An American viewpoint

J. D. McAulay

'The school', wrote John Dewey in 1896, 'is fundamentally an institution erected by society to do a certain specific work.' A study of American educational history strongly supports this generalization. The American people, sensing their uniqueness, have given the school, through its programme, organization and administration, the responsibility of advancing the nation's most cherished ideas.[1] However, unlike Pallas Athena, sprung full-grown from the forehead of Zeus, the public-school system, grades 1 to 12, did not materialize overnight. It evolved from a continuing process of self-revitalization. It expanded from a commitment, on the part of the American people, to the social value of a differential education for the young and to a willingness to finance innovations which could spell the difference between a right and wrong turn.

An Historical Overview

The establishment of the English Classical School in Boston in 1821 initiated the free public secondary school movement.[2] Boys only were admitted. Five years later a similar school for girls was opened in the same city. In 1856, the first coeducational high school was opened in Chicago. However, the legal beginning of the American secondary school, as a distinct institution, dates from the Massachusetts Law of 1827,[3] which required a high school in every town having 500 families. A heavy penalty was attached for failure to comply with the law which was amended in 1835, allowing any smaller town to form a high school as well. The Massachusetts

High School deeply influenced educational developments in other states and established the high school as an institution peculiarly adapted to the needs and wants of the American people.

Pressure for advancing the school leaving age in the United States increased during the period of reconstruction following the Civil War. The black depression resulting from the economic panic of 1873 accelerated this pressure.[4] Labour unions took on a new impetus and joined forces with those who demanded a higher quantity and quality in public education. Particularly, the Noble Order of the Knights of Labor, founded in 1869 and open to all working men, realized that the improvement of the working man's lot might be achieved through a better education.

At the conclusion of the Civil War in 1865 industrialization increased at a rapid pace. Railroads as well as mining, lumber, meat-packing, iron and steel, oil and similar industries expanded operations and accelerated technological know-how. Such expansion and improvement demanded a skilled labour force which could adapt itself to changing industrial techniques and methods. A more efficient and productive labouring class must be an educated one. Industrial management did not oppose, nor did it strongly encourage, the spread of public education.

The constitutionality of the high school and taxation to maintain it was attacked in the courts several times before the Kalamazoo Case of 1872. The city of Kalamazoo, Michigan, in that year voted to establish a high school and employ a superintendent of schools, levying additional school taxes to cover the expense. A citizen by the name of Stuart brought suit to prevent the collection of additional taxes. The case was carried to the Supreme Court of the State of Michigan, in which the decision was reached that 'free schools, in which education, and at their option the elements of classical education, must be brought within reach of all the children of the State'.

Today most of the departments of education in the fifty states of the union have some responsibility to enforce compulsory attendance laws. The early compulsory education laws placed the school leaving age at 13 or 14 years. Today the most frequently reported age at which pupils must begin regular attendance is 7 years and the most frequently stated school leaving age is 16. Thirty-one states of the fifty specify ages 7–16 as the compulsory education age range.[5] In four states 17 years and in five states 18 years is the compulsory school leaving age. However even if a youth leaves school at 16, it is difficult to secure real employment until the age of

18 is reached. The Fair Labor Standards Act of 1940 outlaws child labour in industries engaged in interstate commerce.

It is somewhat remarkable that the public high school grew so rapidly. In theory, from its earliest days, it was open to all the children of all the people. Its programme, in practice, was planned more for the upper ability-level group and actually served better those in a favoured economic position. However, practice did not keep up with theory. From 1910–20 vocational courses were added to the high-school curriculum, particularly agriculture and homemaking. The Smith-Hughes Law of 1917 made Federal funds available to implement these programmes. Students and parents believed these courses were highly practicable. Industrial arts gained status and was offered by more and more schools.

The decade of the 1930s was that of the Great Depression. Expansion of the high-school programme was difficult. Many students found it difficult or impossible to remain in school because of Depression conditions. The Federal Government enacted laws to aid youth. The National Youth Administration Act (N.Y.A.) provided funds to pay high-school students for useful work performed under the direction of the school. The Civilian Conservation Camp afforded work opportunities for young men under semi-military living and working conditions. Many persons feared that the Federal Government was assuming the direction and control of the nation's secondary education programme.

The decade of the 1940s influenced the complexion of secondary education through the impact of World War II. Courses were added to the secondary-school curriculum which would be helpful in promoting scientific knowledge. Students and teachers engaged extensively in civic jobs designed to promote the effective prosecution of the war. Following the war a close look was given the high-school curriculum, particularly on that part which served as a terminal education for about 60% of the enrolment. This concern took the form of a new movement entitled 'Life Adjustment Education', which attempted to make the normal high-school programme function effectively in the lives of the students.

During the decade of the 1950s secondary education was the beneficiary of much experimentation. Programmes for slow-learning and gifted students received widespread attention. Resources for use as aids to learning multiplied. Dr James Bryant Conant, President Emeritus of Harvard University, made a study of the American high school under the auspices of the Carnegie Corporation. Many of the Conant recommendations became noticeable as part of the secondary-school programme in the 1960s. Some of them are as follows: ability grouping by subjects; elective subjects to meet the needs and interest of all students; adequate counselling service; emphasis on English composition; sufficient study of modern foreign languages to attain speaking fluency; recognition of achievement by the academically talented; organizing schools of such size as to have 100 or more in the graduating class; and electing a good Board of Education to determine school policies.

The future of secondary education is exciting, but questionable. How student and teacher militancy, increasing educational technological and Federal funding will influence secondary education is a matter of conjecture and concern.

Socio-economic Aspects of the School Leaving Age

'Education', said John F. Kennedy, 'is a means of developing our greatest abilities because in each of us there is a private hope and dream which, fulfilled, can be translated into benefits for everyone and greater strength for our nation.'[6] It has been estimated that in recent years America's investment in education has been responsible for up to 40 per cent of the nation's growth and productivity.[7] It is an investment which results in higher wages and greater purchasing power for the worker and in the new products and techniques which come from trained minds. Our past industrial revolution has accelerated the demand for better educated, more competent citizens.

During the past ten years, 50,000 elevator jobs disappeared in New York City alone – 8,000 during the last year. As more elevators become automatically operated, fewer and fewer unskilled and semi-skilled workers will be needed. A person with normal intelligence can learn how to operate an elevator after two days of instruction. Another example is the 'Gandy Dancers', railroad workers who lay ballast and ties and then put the track down. They get their name from the peculiar way they walk over the ties as they carry the track. Today modern machinery can lay the same amount of track as 100 men did before. The main requirement for 'Gandy Dancers' used to be a good, strong back: today companies require a high school diploma. The Sylvania Electric Company has introduced automated examining equipment for the purpose of checking transistors, so that today four men can do the work 100 did a few years ago.[8]

Cheques today contain numerals printed peculiarly at the bottom or top. These are magnetic tape numbers. Less than two years ago very few cheques were so imprinted. This means that cheques sorting can be done and is done by machines. A new machine recently introduced into banks has radically reduced the number of bank tellers. A deposit is fed into a machine. Each item is separated – cheques, bills, coins – and photographed. A receipted slip is then returned to the depositor.

Such advance in technology and automation would seem to erase job opportunities. Certainly the types and kinds of jobs as we knew them are disappearing, but not the number. The A.F.L.-C.I.O. predicts that for every 100 skilled jobs in 1955 there are today some 150 such jobs.

This demand for skilled competencies has kept our young people in school for a longer period of time. Thirty years ago only 302 students graduated out of every 1,000 who entered high school. Today the high school has doubled its holding power and tripled its college-going rate. Thirty years ago two out of three students dropped out of high school. Today one out of four drops out. Parents have learned that remaining in school will give the child future financial advantages.[9]

If you complete	You can expect a median income of $
Less than 8 years of schooling	2,090
8 years of schooling	3,452
1–3 years of high school	3,865
4 years of high school	5,052
1–3 years of college	5,246
4 years of college	7,261
1 or more years of graduate school	7,691

However, if the child is to remain in school beyond the fifteenth or sixteenth year his education must be meaningful and have relevancy. For example, it is useless for a young person to remain in school to learn the skills of a key-punch operator. Such operators have been superseded by machines and have been declared surplus by the California Employment Service. However, today five vocational schools in Los Angeles advertise that they train key-punch operators.[10]

A dozen years ago a British group known as the Archbishop of Canterbury's Fifth Committee made the following statement: 'A nation which regards education primarily as a means of converting its members into more efficient instruments of production is likely not only to jeopardize its moral standards and educational ideals, but to discover that by such methods it cannot attain even the limited success at which it aims.' The object of education is not only manpower, but manhood as well. What education can and must do is help people become human.

The young person who stays on in school for an extra year must not be narrowly trained, but so educated that he is ready for anything. He must be prepared for the human use of his free time, inspired to desire for life-long learning and supplied with that training which will make it possible. The youth who stays on in school must be supplied with the intellectual tools, the intellectual discipline and the intellectual framework which will help him understand the ever-increasing problems society must face. The Chief of Police of the City of Chicago underscored this educational objective when requesting a 'completely professionalized force'. He said: 'This professionalism must be based on a foundation of intellectual attainment. It is necessary to secure a complete man who has an understanding of his society and its people – a sense of perspective that can only come from a knowledge of history and philosophy.' Perhaps the most practical education is a theoretical one, because the man with a theoretical framework will comprehend the new situation, whereas the man without it has no recourse but to muddle through. Unfortunately, there is a widespread tendency to think of extra years of schooling as more or less interchangeable from one community to the next and to believe they can be measured by a fixed standard, such as the percentage who go on to college. Rather, the standard of progress should be moving towards goals set by the needs of the individual, the domestic economy and international demands facing the nation – a standard moving towards even higher goals of quality.

The secondary schools, therefore, must, of course, be designed to prepare young people for a broad variety of college programmes. But they must also provide adequate training opportunities for the millions of young people now in the lower schools who will enter the labour market without a college degree in the 1970s. These young people must receive the kind of education and training opportunities suited to the changing times. They must be so prepared that they will plan for further education and re-education when their skills and technical knowledge must be updated or when their jobs disappear because of automation and economic change.

An American viewpoint 123

When President Johnson said that 'the first work of these times and the first work of our society is education', he was expressing a growing popular belief as much as he was characterizing his own Administration. Every society and every generation within that society produces forces that mould education in its time. What seems to be emerging in our society and within our generation is a widespread faith that if we can improve and extend education we might save and improve not only the society, but civilization as well.

Social change is of such rapid acceleration that the very fabric of society threatens to be torn asunder. The change includes our transition from a country to a city way of life as well as a rapid mechanization and automation of industry. Time and space have been conquered by modern miracles of communication and transportation. The surging growth of population, the development of hideous means of destruction and the centralization of power in gigantic institutions threaten to destroy the foundations of our society. The development of unthinkably frightful weapons of war and the use of alternative social and political systems, apparently in permanent irreconcilable conflict with our own, confuses and worries the average citizen. The rapid shift in occupational structure and the sudden obsolescence of many vocations frightens him.

Such social changes have created a modification of our political processes and new interpretation of law. Scientific techniques of measuring and influencing opinion have transformed elections. National and worldwide developments have triggered insistent demands by coloured people for an equal share in material prosperity. Erupting demands for political, economic and social justice have quickened national life and unsettled social relationships. With these changes has come such a rapid extension of knowledge that the most sensitive and well-informed are humbled by their own inadequacies of understanding.[11]

Only an educated mind can adjust to such social change. Barbara Ward, the eminent British economist, wrote:

> The human heart has both appetites and despairs which rational codes alone are unable to control. Man is lonely. He is not self-sufficient. He rebels against meaninglessness in life. He is haunted by death. He is afraid. He needs to feel himself part of a wider whole and he has unassuageable powers of dedication and devotion which must find expression in worship and service. . . . In times of crisis, when insecurity, anxiety, loneliness and the meaninglessness of life become well nigh

insupportable . . . the hunger for godlike leadership, for religious assurance, for a merging of the self in the security of the whole becomes irresistible.[12]

The very marginality of today's youth and the frightful conflicts and choices adolescents face in a crisis-ridden world heightens their need for that schooling which will prepare them for fearlessness and freedom, for responsibility and creativity. The vast majority of our youth reside in an urban society where there is a frank confrontation of value conflicts prevalent in American society today. City youth requires a different schooling than does his rural cousin, in that an urban nation such as ours requires different standards and behaviour of its youth than does a rural society. In an urban society people live much closer together and its youth must be taught co-operation, patience and human understanding. In a rural society youth has much space in which to wander. There are few 'No Trespassing' signs, few properties where children are not welcome. In a rural society there is real work for the young to do – not made work. There is honest responsibility and necessary physical work. There is sufficient space where one can expand without damaging anyone. A youth within an urban setting must receive an education which will prepare him for city life.

City life does give the child some educational advantages and the opportunity to learn from his surroundings. He can acquire so much more information through the eye and the ear and the senses and so little by actual doing in the city environment as compared to a rural one that the problem of utilizing excess leisure time in profitable activities has become a most serious one for social and educational leaders. Under urban conditions of living, the youth must assume greater initiative and responsibility and self-discipline. With the growing concentration of industry and business in the hands of a few giant corporations, with the virtual abolition of apprenticeship and the increasing trend for skilled and specialized labour in our society today, youth are caught in several false educational assumptions which further compound their difficulties.[13]

The Dilemma of Today's Youth

Many people believe that youth are constitutionally opposed to learning and it is a waste of taxpayers' money to further educate it. The belief that youth do not want to learn is disputed by the very nature of learning. Learning is an integral part of growth. It is a product of experience. Learning is a continuous experience. Learning leads to more learning as the purposive human organism develops and adjusts to its environment. On the other hand, there are many who believe a youth can learn anything if he tries. This may be the basis for our culture placing such a high value on the classical academic curriculum to which many of our young cannot adapt because of their individual uniqueness. Thus the argument is made: if a child cannot adjust to and learn from the school's ordained curriculum he should be ignored. School is not for him, because he is not worthy of an education.

Many believe that democracy will not work in our schools. Unfortunately, many teachers hold this belief. They confess they have tried democracy in the classroom, but it was not successful. Such teachers resort to those methods which reach immediate goals, such as a quiet room with every student making notes from a text. Such methods choke any possibility for significant learning to take place in the classroom. When the teacher indicates the students are under control, he often means the classroom is adult-centred and in complete authority. But if a child has completed eight to ten years of schooling without having experienced a democratic classroom he may have some difficulty at 15 making democratic decisions. Democracy is a way of life in which individuals consult with each other on a basis of mutual respect. A group of 15-year-olds may have problems learning to live and work together because they have never experienced mutual respect. The democratic way of life must permeate the lower grades, so that when the youth reaches adolescence he will be at home in a democratic atmosphere. He will know how to behave with self-discipline based on a strong moral fibre.

Some believe that no learning can take place without pain. Thus there is resentment when young people are enjoying themselves at school. Such persons believe the modern school contains too many frills. Many secondary schools contain courses whose sole objective is that it is good for youth to suffer. It is believed that academic courses are hard, but vocational courses are easy. However, a course in higher mathematics may be quite essential and delectable to some students, but completely useless and repugnant to others. The school, to be inviting to all youth, must not only be physically comfortable and pleasant, but also have broad opportunities and activities.

Hardness for the sake of hardness is contradictory to education and the development of a free human organism. Today's urban youth have learned that modern technology not only makes production more efficient, but more pleasant as well. They will not buy an educational programme simply because it is hard.

Many of today's youth are caught in the dilemma of the old curriculum consisting of such courses as English, history, science, foreign language and mathematics, which many believe are in themselves educative. These subjects become the rocks upon which many a youth is broken. Such youth need different facilitating experiences, those which will give them courage to face and solve unique dilemmas, to be conscious of the needs of others and to establish one's self-integrity.

There is the belief that it is possible to determine early who is able and to separate them out from the rest for further schooling. Great dependability is placed in the I.Q. test as an instrument for such selection. The assumption is made that the brighter a person is the more difficult his academic work should be. Much faith is placed in the deluge of tests flooding our schools. It is believed they will separate the gifted from the less able. But individual children mature at different ages and at different rates. Tests alone will not detect potentialities. This varying rate of development is especially true in adolescence. Youth should be so taught that the potentialities of each learner can be properly developed. They should be taught those skills which will help them work with others. Preparation for college is not the only desirable objective of the secondary school.

Each human being is significantly unique, and Nature went to an enormous amount of trouble to bring about this uniqueness. Each young person is built out of unique experiences, unique purposes and unique perceptions. Such knowledge as he possesses is unlike that of any other. It is related to an unique personality. Modern society, however, is determined on standardization of personality and behaviour, even though uniqueness is an individual's most valuable asset. The young person's differences in personality from others is his reasons to be. No child is expendable. Every child has something, knows something which nobody else has or knows. Great emotional pressures would be removed from today's youth if the scientific fact were accepted that each human body is unique.

Too, there is the perpetual complaint that young people today are not establishing and maintaining standards. Maintaining standards has broken many young people and embittered many teachers. Too many adults set standards which are outside the learner. Students are exhorted and coerced to learn, in the name of standards, that which they are not willing or able to study. Thus standards are maintained by lowering grades and increasing homework. Perhaps the abandonment of the belief that subject matter is a good in itself, even though subject matter is essential to the learning process, would lessen the emotional strain of today's youth.

Humanizing education does not necessarily mean the abandonment of standards. If the concept is abandoned that all youth have to learn the same things and that it is possible to have different standards for different people, many young people will have less difficulty in school. Every child should have the opportunity to develop his own individual potentialities, so that the full meaning of being human can emerge.

There is a common assumption abroad that the mind is something separate from the body and can be trained independently. A youth is expected to sit quietly in a classroom, paying attention to and concentrating on only his books or the words of the teacher. The next period he moves to the gymnasium, where his body is to be trained. Supposedly he does not use his body in the classroom nor his mind in the gymnasium. Mind and body are treated as separate entities, even though medical science has long since proved that no mental illness exists without a physical cause. Man is the only animal that has the wonderful ability to think, to use intelligence in the solution of unpredictable problems. This is man's most priceless possession and its development must be the primary purpose of education. This cannot be accomplished by merely reading or listening to the thoughts of others. Young people today demand physical, mental and emotional involvement with the physical world about them.

They want to know how to adjust to other human beings and to novel situations, because they realize they cannot survive in our closely knit society without this knowledge, which cannot be learned in a vacuum. Adjusting to other people and to the situation in which one finds himself is probably the most important learning anyone ever achieves. The young person must learn how to maintain himself in a way to satisfy his ego and at the same time conduct himself in a manner that will draw other people to him for mutual development. Many youth in our urban culture are mentally ill because of the inability to adjust to modern society. Mass communication and transportation tend to promote conformity. Today's youth has indeed a difficult row to hoe.

What causes School Failure?

Many studies on drop-outs show that the mean intelligence quotients of drop-outs are lower than school stay-ins. However, one study completed by the U.S. Department of Labor indicated 6 per cent of the drop-outs had I.Q.s over 110.[14] In another study completed in New York State 12 per cent of the drop-outs had I.Q.s above 110.[15] Thus many children who drop out of school have the ability not only to graduate from high school, but also to graduate from college. Why do they fail?

The location of the school seems to be partially responsible. Urban and rural areas have the highest rates of school drop-outs. Suburbia has the least. One large American city, which has an annual city-wide drop-out rate in senior high school of less than 10 per cent, has a range of drop-outs for individual schools from 4 per cent to 26 per cent. This means that in one school, one out of every four students disappears from the classroom during the school year.

The drop-out rate is influenced by the distance from home to school. Too, the family attitudes towards school and education in general, plus the motivation a child receives at home, is important as to whether he graduates from school or not. Two separate studies, one by Dr A. L. Bertrand in Louisiana and another by Dr James Moore in New York, indicated two-thirds of the parents of drop-outs had negative or indifferent attitudes towards school. Such parents believed that a high-school education would not be a deterrent in earning a living. However, almost 100 per cent of the parents of the school stay-ins believe a young person would be seriously handicapped if he did not possess a high-school education. Parental attitude and involvement is a most important factor affecting the young person's desire to finish a high-school education.

To keep children in school, teachers must make contact with them. Students are motivated when they feel the teacher knows them, recognizes them as persons, listens to them, gives them ideas and is always willing to help them.[16] The teacher develops good relations with students when he recognizes each individual and identifies with that individual. Such recognition and identification help the student to develop a powerful feeling of self-respect. The knowledge that a teacher cares may be the single contributing reason for the student remaining in school.

Bad relations between home and school may cause a child's early drop-out. The school exists to help the young, and this can only be done if there are positive relationships between home and school. The accessibility of administrators and teachers to parents must be increased. A principal should free himself for one morning a week, so that he is accessible to see parents whose children are contemplating leaving school. Teachers also should make themselves increasingly available to talk with parents. A note, telephone call, or simple invitation to come in for a talk is greatly appreciated by a disturbed parent. Accessibility days or hours may provide an opportunity for teachers and parents jointly to plan ways of supporting each other and of gaining deeper insights into a child's feelings, concerns and performances related to school.

Teachers and administrators should emphasize the importance of having local groups invest time and resources to determine why young people leave school. Studies should be undertaken designed to identify the concerns and needs of children and youth. Emphasis might be given to the continued assessment of the outcomes of the educational programme. Such evaluation and study provide teacher and pupil with specific information concerning what is happening to children in a given community, and gives a revelation of the characteristics of local youth in terms of health factors, recreational interests, activities, work responsibilities, participation in sports and participation in cultural activities. Such assessment would feed into the school vital current and useful information which could become a basis of action in the prevention of school dropouts.

A Suitable Curriculum for the Extra Year

A curriculum is that part of the school programme specifically designed to provide planned learning experiences for the youth in the school. To hold young people in school, the curriculum must emphasize individual achievement as its central purpose. If the school accepts as one of its goals the development in its pupils of individual attitudes and skills that will lead to a worthy use of leisure-time, then those experiences will be organized into the curriculum, which will assist young people to develop such attitudes and skills.

But the curriculum must also be related to limitations imposed by legal authority. In many states minimum curricula have been imposed on schools. Physical education, for example, is usually required of all pupils attending public schools. From one to four years of English is often a state requirement. Some states prescribe a considerable portion of the curriculum content. Too, the curriculum must be related to the particular needs of the community. Communities differ economically, socially, politically and culturally. They possess different traditions, different heritages and different mores. Some communities are ethnically relatively homogeneous.

Others are strange admixtures of unassimilated ethnic groups. But there is also a sameness among communities. There is usually a common language and a common form of government. Increased mobility of population has developed a trend towards sameness. In a community where many young people must work after school to help the family, the organization of the curriculum will probably be quite different from that of a community where few of the students find it necessary to work after school. At the same time, the curriculum must provide common learning experiences which will help the young to live intelligently in any community in the country. The curriculum must assume the task of adjusting the old and the new cultural elements, thereby achieving a synthesis that forms the bases of the society in which the youngster lives.

School-size imposes certain limitations on the curriculum. Small schools cannot provide the range of learning experiences available in larger schools. Conant[17] concluded in his study of American high schools that the enrolment in many American secondary schools is too small to permit a broad diversified curriculum. He felt that such small secondary schools operate against economical, quality education and they are wasteful of the time and talents of administrators and teachers. At the same time the curriculum must be directly related to the ability and desire of the community to pay for its schools. To develop a curriculum that the community cannot afford is to invite frustration. However, to develop a curriculum that involves less cost than the community is willing to assume is to deprive children of that which the community is willing to give them. It is not the responsibility of the school to save money, but rather to spend most wisely the money the taxpayers are willing to spend. The buildings and equipment that are available will be dependent to a large extent on the financial support offered by the community. For the learning experience involved in the curriculum, proper buildings, equipment and facilities must be available.

The modern educational curriculum is the result of many interests, social pressures and situations, in which many individuals, organizations and institutions of community and national scope have participated. In a dynamic, democratic society, communities and public education are destined to change. These changes must be consistent and compatible with the best interests of those who are to be educated and will be reflected in the curriculum.

The chief function of the school is to improve and to extend the quantity and quality of learning by providing experiences, through the curriculum, which will make a maximum contribution to the education of boys and girls. To facilitate the integration of learning experiences the curriculum might be divided into five content areas:[18]

> Area A: English, social studies (history, geography, economics or anthropology).
> Area B: mathematics and science.
> Area C: fine arts (music, art, dramatics).
> Area D: practical arts (industrial arts, home-making and business education).
> Area E: physical education and health.

In developing this curriculum teachers, with consultants, should determine the content in the various subject fields, such as English, mathematics, social studies, science, etc. This completed, area meetings are held during which English and social studies, mathematics and science, music and art and the other curriculum areas listed above are integrated wherever possible. This is followed by meetings between areas (A meets with B, C with D, etc.) in order to effect further integration, until, in fact as well as in intent, the entire curriculum is integrated. Each content area should be 'purpose-centred'.

For example, the purposes for the teaching of English should involve teachers, citizens in the community, the administration and consultants. These purposes then become part of the sum total of purposes of the school, provided that they fit into the framework of the overall purposes and philosophy of the school. Those teachers and consultants developing the English curriculum should select only that content which contributes towards the achievement of specific purposes. That content, even though it be traditional, is omitted if it does not contribute to these purposes. The English group can then organize the content of the English curriculum in a sequence that seems to best meet the needs of the young people.

This curriculum in English might be organized in terms of particular years of English, rather than specific courses in English. It might be quite possible for a student of a specific age to need English experiences usually met at another age level. This curriculum should be so organized that it is possible for this young person to study English at whatever level his need is pertinent. The sequence of curriculum content is organized on the basis of what each young person requires rather than in terms of a set structure into which each young person must fit regardless of his ability and background. Thus the curriculum is developed for each child, rather than placing a child into a prescribed curriculum. The rapid advancement of technology in education allows the organization for such a curriculum.

Skills, knowledge and understandings in each of the subject fields can be identified and then coded for use on an I.B.M. card. Again using English as an example, the skills (listed sequentially) that a particular student does not possess are punched on the student's card. The cards are run through a sorter, which groups students on the basis of English skills they have not yet mastered. Such groups can be organized into classes and assigned to teachers who have been made aware of these students' English needs. Thus an English curriculum has been organized for each student, each student taught in groups of varying sizes.

The content for each subject field is developed in two parts; one part of the content all students should experience. Another part of the content should be available only to those students who need it or want it.

The important aspect of such a curriculum organization is that the student's progress and achievement is measured in terms of what he has learned rather than the number of courses he has passed. A perusal of the student's I.B.M. card will reveal quickly what he has learned and what remains to be learned. Students within a particular class will be given the opportunity to progress at their own speeds.

The teacher's principal responsibility is to be concerned with individual differences within the classroom. Each student must be encouraged and stimulated to learn as much as he is capable of learning. As each term ends, the individual student is re-scheduled on the basis of his progress during the past term. Under ideal learning conditions there would be constant evaluation of a student's work, and as he gained understanding and skill he would be regrouped into another class. It is possible to place in sequence all of the experiences to which pupils are exposed in each subject field. That curriculum which will retain young people in school is committed to a real consideration of differences among individuals. That curriculum which has meaning and value makes it possible for teachers to provide an individual programme for each young person.

Conclusion

As at present organized and patterned, the hard truth is that many of our schools honestly promote the objective of discouraging a young person from remaining in school. Rather than offering assistance and stimulation to develop their own individuality within the school environment, many young people are locked into a regimented system that attempts to stamp them all in the same mould. The student is filled with facts and figures which only accidentally and too infrequently have anything to do with the problems and conflicts of modern life or his own inner concern.[19] What many young people need and want are matters of no apparent interest to anyone associated with the schools. Many students see school as Rilke describes it.[20]

> The time of school drags by with waiting
> And dread, with nothing but dreary things.
> O loneliness, O leaden waiting out of time.

What is taught, how it is taught, and when and where it is taught must not be based on the needs and convenience of the school, upon the comfort of the administrators or the logistics of the system. To retain youth in school the programme must have meaning for those who attend.

REFERENCES

1 See Educational Policies Commission, *Public Education and the Future of America*, Washington, D.C., National Education Association, 1955.

2 Samford, Clarence D., et al., *Secondary Education*, William C. Brown Co., 1963, p. 17.

3 Cubberley, Ellwood, *Public Education in the United States*, Houghton Mifflin Co., 1934, p. 257.

4 Nevins, Alan and Commager, Henry Steele, *A Pocket History of the United States*, New York: Washington Square Press, Inc., 1966, p. 283.

5 Knezevich, Stephen J., *Administration of Public Education*, Harper & Brothers, 1962, p. 342.

6 Kennedy, John F., President of the United States, *New York Times*, 30 July 1961.

7 Keppel, Francis, 'The Kind of Public Schools We Want', in *Contemporary Thoughts on Public School Curriculum*, ed. E. C. Short and G. D. Marconnit, William C. Brown Co., 1968, p. 77.

8 Schreiber, Daniel, 'The School Dropout – Fugitive from Failure', *The Bulletin*, National Association of Secondary School Principals, 46, No. 274, May 1966, p. 81.

9 Statistical, *Summary of Education*, U.S. Department of Health, Education and Welfare, Washington, D.C., 1969.

10 Hutchins, Robert Maynard, 'Are we Educating our Children for the Wrong Future?' *Saturday Review*, 11 September 1965, p. 83.

11 McCreary, Eugene, 'Schools for Fearlessness and Freedom', *Phi Delta Kappan*, 46, February 1965, p. 258.

12 Ward, Barbara, *Faith and Freedom*, Image paper-back, Garden City, New York: Doubleday, 1958, p. 67.
13 Kelley, Earl C., *In defence of Youth*, Prentice Hall, 1962, p. 101.
14 U.S. Department of Labor, *From School to Work*, March 1960.
15 Woollatt, L. H., 'Why Capable Students drop out of School', *N.A.S.S.P. Bulletin*, November 1961, p. 87.
16 Doll, Ronald C., and Fleming, Robert S., *Children Under Pressure*, Charles E. Merrill, 1966, p. 92.
17 Conant, James Bryant, *The American High School Today*, New York: McGraw-Hill Book Co., Inc., 1959, p. 77.
18 Rollins, Sidney P., and Unrich, Adolph, *Introduction to Secondary Education*, Chicago: Rand McNally & Co., 1964, p. 63.
19 Noyes, Kathryn Johnson and McAndrew, Gordon L., 'Is this what Schools are for?', *Saturday Review*, 21 December 1968, p. 65.
20 Rilke, Rainer Maria, 'Childhood'.

For Product Safety Concerns and Information please contact our EU representative GPSR@taylorandfrancis.com
Taylor & Francis Verlag GmbH, Kaufingerstraße 24, 80331 München, Germany

www.ingramcontent.com/pod-product-compliance
Lightning Source LLC
Chambersburg PA
CBHW061416300426
44114CB00015B/1962